Transforming Teacher Education

'This book is an insightful and highly readable analysis of the work of teacher educators in England, but its value extends far beyond that setting. Combining original studies of teacher educators with trenchant critique of education policy trends in England and elsewhere, this book is a must-read for those who reject the "defend or reform" dichotomy and instead want genuine transformation of teacher education.' **Marilyn Cochran-Smith, Cawthorne Professor of Teacher Education for Urban Schools, Lynch School of Education, Boston College, USA**

'This excellent book is a very timely and insightful analysis of some of the consequences – both intended and unintended – arising out of a time of unprecedented change in the teacher education sector.' **Samantha Twiselton, Director of Sheffield Institute of Education, Sheffield Hallam University, UK**

'In this thoughtful volume, Viv Ellis and Jane McNicholl offer a deliberate plan for the transformation of initial teacher education. *Transforming Teacher Education* represents a vision that neither defends nor reforms but uncompromisingly takes bold steps towards collaboration and collective creativity, a vision for remaking initial teacher education such that another future for our work is possible – not just in England but elsewhere in the world too.' **A. Lin Goodwin, Vice Dean and Evenden Professor of Education, Teachers College, Columbia University, USA**

'The politics of teacher education have been destabilized in most countries, often resulting in derisory discussion of both teachers and teacher educators. This book provides a helpful framework to think pro-actively about teacher education as a field and offers a seriously challenging agenda for transforming that field of practice. It considers the much neglected daily work of teacher educators and their positioning in higher education institutions and comes up with an important agenda in which public universities and the profession might better work together to develop and change the practices of teacher education. Such a provocative agenda offers the potential for researchers and practitioners in many countries to build both scholarship and practice in ways that invite multilateral international networks to develop.' **Marie Brennan, Professor of Education, Victoria University, Melbourne, Australia**

'Written by authors with a deep understanding of developments in teacher education, *Transforming Teacher Education* is a timely and important book that captures the complexity of the work of teacher educators. Based on their extensive research and offering a transformative agenda, it is an important source for practitioners, managers and policymakers who are dedicated to transform teacher education and improve the work and academic status of all those who work within the field.' **Anja Swennen, Researcher and Teacher Educator, Faculty of Psychology and Pedagogy, VU University Amsterdam, The Netherlands**

'This is an important book. The authors offer a rich, complex and detailed approach to an alternative "transforming" perspective, drawing upon a wide range of theory and research which they link to practical outcomes. They have put forward versions of this analysis at conferences in different countries – notably the USA and the UK where the neoliberal alternative to "transformation" has been prominent – but now the publication of the book can provide teachers and scholars with a substantial basis that will enable them to review and build on these constructive ideas in their own work.' **Brian Street, Professor Emeritus of Language and Education, King's College London, UK**

Transforming
Teacher Education:

Reconfiguring the Academic Work

**BY VIV ELLIS
AND JANE MCNICHOLL**

Bloomsbury Academic
An imprint of Bloomsbury Publishing Plc

B L O O M S B U R Y
LONDON · NEW DELHI · NEW YORK · SYDNEY

Bloomsbury Academic

An imprint of Bloomsbury Publishing Plc

50 Bedford Square	1385 Broadway
London	New York
WC1B 3DP	NY 10018
UK	USA

www.bloomsbury.com

BLOOMSBURY and the Diana logo are trademarks of Bloomsbury Publishing Plc

First published 2015

© Viv Ellis and Jane McNicholl, 2015

British Library Cataloguing-in-Publication Data
A catalogue record for this book is available from the British Library.

ISBN: HB: 978-1-4725-0884-3
PB: 978-1-4725-0720-4
ePDF: 978-1-4725-0639-9
ePub: 978-1-4725-1184-3

Library of Congress Cataloging-in-Publication Data
A catalog record for this book is available from the Library of Congress.

Typeset by Integra Software Services Pvt. Ltd
Printed and bound in Great Britain

Contents

Preface

This book is about how we educate, train and develop teachers and, specifically, about higher education's contribution to their preparation. We researched and wrote the book over the 4 years since the election of a Conservative-Liberal Democrat coalition government in the UK in 2010. Our interests in transforming teacher education pre-date this election but the rhetoric of reform since 2010 has spurred us on to complete our investigations, go through the processes of peer review, search the international research literature, make site visits to several countries and submit a proposal to Bloomsbury that has led to this book. The book will be published a few months before the 2015 General Election in the UK and at about the same time as the Carter Review of Initial Teacher Education reports (the Carter Review is an independent but government-initiated and supported review of the content of initial teacher education programmes in England; see https://www.gov.uk/government/news/new-advisory-group-to-support-initial-teacher-training-review). Whether we like it or not, the book comes out of a political context and it will feed into one. So right at the beginning of the book we want to signal that we are not writing it to be defensive of the *status quo* in initial teacher education in England or anywhere else. We are not seeking simply to defend what has gone on in universities under the name of initial teacher preparation.

When talking about education and education policy it has become very common to fall into a familiar rhetorical trap. Neoliberalism and the specific policy turn that Stephen Ball (e.g. 2012) has termed the Global Education Reform Movement – the GERM – presents urgent arguments in the public sphere that are presented as 'reform' ideas. They are strongly and explicitly motivated and often articulated with great eloquence and fervour. These reform ideas frame proposals that have easily recognizable and often apparently well-intentioned outcomes and the outcomes are measurable through the specification of targets and numerical benchmarks. The modality of reform is one that has become known as New Public Management (McLaughlin et al. 2002). The trap for those who have an alternative view is one of simply defending current arrangements, of arguing that there is evidence that these arrangements are sufficient and that the risks associated with the reforms are too high. Statistics and methodological critiques are often traded in skirmishes, the terms of which have already been set by the reformers. The GERM has determined the ground on which the argument takes place, its premises, propositions and overall conclusions.

Debates about teacher education have often followed this pattern and we discuss some of the reasons for this situation in the chapters that follow. In summary, we believe that teacher education as a field within the discipline of Education has been somewhat conservative in approaching its own development as a higher education activity. In this book, we refer principally to the UK (specifically, England) but we do believe the argument has wider relevance internationally. However, it is important to note we do not seek to blame teacher educators for this situation nor to apportion blame elsewhere. Rather, we seek to offer an analysis of the situation as it has arisen culturally and historically and then to propose some ideas for the development of the field that will be of benefit to the education system as whole as well as to the academic discipline. So we do not defend teacher education as it is in this book. Instead, we want to work towards a transformative agenda.

Our rejection of the reform/defend dichotomy and our commitment to the transformation of existing arrangements have been stimulated by the work of many scholars. Pauline Lipman's 2011 book *The New Political Economy of Urban Education* was particularly influential. Writing about urban education and about Chicago schools in particular, Lipman argued for the necessity of 'rupturing the neoliberal tropes that opposition means supporting the *status quo*' (Lipman 2011, p. 164). In place of a defensive stance, Lipman proposed a transformative one that opened out the debate to the wider society and engaged children, parents and communities. She proposed a category of 'nonreformist reforms' that intervened in the ruptures between reformist and defensive positions. Fundamentally, she argued for a reframing of the arguments as a first step in 'fracturing the hegemonic alliance' that supports the GERM, asserting that 'how issues are framed sets the parameters of possible solutions, defines who is responsible, and embodies the sort of society we wish to have' (p. 163). Cognitive linguist George Lakoff has made many similar arguments for reframing the arguments of 'left' and 'right' in our general politics (e.g. Lakoff 2004). No matter how much 'data' or 'evidence' one produces from defensive standpoint, the power of the reformers' framing metaphor is determining.

Viv Ellis rehearsed the argument we have started to make here at a seminar at the University of Washington in April 2012 (Ellis 2012a), strongly influenced by Lipman's work and against a background of a growing crisis in teacher education – and higher education – in England. The analysis of the reform/defend dichotomy in teacher education policy and proposals for a transformative reframing have subsequently been made elsewhere (e.g. Zeichner & Sandoval 2013). We believe we need more than a critical sociology of teacher education policy and an awareness of the hegemonic alliance and funding networks that underpin GERM rhetoric about the preparation of teachers. If teacher education is also an educational project and one driven by educational questions, then we also need a pedagogical analysis of the situation that is future oriented and simultaneously both theoretical and practical. The goal of this book is to arrive at a pedagogical agenda for the transformation of teacher education – not to present a completed recipe for 'rolling out' or 'scaling up', as the pervasive metaphors of reform might have it. To that extent, we are almost setting out to write a book that will be unsatisfactory by currently dominant criteria. If, however, we at least begin to stimulate a reframing of the arguments and identify the ruptures in the reform/defend contradiction in which human agency and creativity might be possible, it will have been worth the effort.

Acknowledgements

The research upon which this book is based was supported by several organizations. The 'Developing English Teaching and Internship Learning (DETAIL)' project (led by Viv Ellis) was funded by the John Fell Fund at the University of Oxford. Viv Ellis would like to thank the trustees of this fund and the teachers who also co-led the project – Nicole Dingwall, Deb Davies, Chris Childs and Kate Spencer-Ellis. 'The Work of Teacher Education' research (Ellis with co-investigators Jane McNicholl, Allan Blake and Jim McNally) was funded by the UK Higher Education Academy with support-in-kind from the Department of Education at the University of Oxford. The 'Pedagogies of Teacher Education for Urban Schools' study was funded by the British Academy (Ellis with co-investigator Meg Maguire) and involved collaborations with Tom Are Trippestad, Yang Xiaowei and Ken Zeichner that have extended beyond the life of the project. Together, we would like to thank the funders who have made the research possible and the collaborators who have stimulated our thinking and provided constructive criticism. Relatively modest amounts of funding over several years have enabled us both to gather the evidence for the arguments we present here.

Support in making practical arrangements for the research and then in preparing the manuscript was provided by Phil Richards and David Griffiths at the University of Oxford and Gary Dear and Christine Preston at Brunel University. Viv Ellis would like to thank Robert Jones, Headteacher of Haydon School; Rachel McDonald, Director of the Guru Nanak Teaching School Alliance; David Poole, Director of the Hillingdon Teaching School Alliance; Collette Richardson, Headteacher of St Matthew's Primary School, all of whom have sustained impressive levels of stamina and resilience in listening to the rehearsal of many of the ideas in the final chapter of this book over the best part of a year. Viv Ellis would also like to thank Gert Biesta who, in addition to being one of the most kind and generous colleagues anyone could hope for, helped to inform some of the arguments in Chapter 6 at a time when words literally failed us.

Anna Pendry was a key influence in the formation of our initial ideas for the 'Work of Teacher Education' study – we began the research with her just prior to her retirement and the high standards she set for empirical investigations continued to influence the way we generated and analysed data. We also wish to acknowledge the friendship and support of Ann Childs at the University of Oxford for her ongoing critical engagement with our research – and her patience. We have both worked with John Furlong and have benefitted from several robust conversations with him about the future of university involvement in teacher education. His 2013 book *Education – The Anatomy of a Discipline* was an important statement of several key ideas and one that we return to throughout this volume. Joce Nuttall and Marie Brennan have both stimulated us to think harder in the way that they have taken up some of our research questions in Australia. *Terms of Work for Composition*, Bruce Horner's 2000 book about the work of teachers of writing in American universities, was also a brilliant and energizing influence on our own thinking.

Sections of Chapters 2 and 5 first appeared in 'Institutional conceptualisations of teacher education as academic work in England' by Viv Ellis, Jane McNicholl and Anna Pendry, published in 2012 in *Teaching and Teacher Education* 28, 5: 685–693, reproduced here with permission of the editors and publishers. Sections of Chapters 3 and 5 first appeared in 'Academic Work and Proletarianisation: A Study of Higher Education-based Teacher Educators' by Viv Ellis, Jane McNicholl, Allan Blake and Jim McNally, published in 2014 in *Teaching and Teacher Education* 40, 3: 33–43, again included with permission of the editors and publishers. One section of Chapter 5 appeared in longer form in 'Living with ghosts: "Disciplines", envy and the future of teacher education' by Viv Ellis, published in 2012 in *Changing English: Studies in Culture and Education* 19, 3: 155–166, and it is reproduced with permission.

The quotation from the play *Prin* by Andrew Davies (published by Samuel French Ltd. in 1989) is reproduced with kind permission of Andrew Davies and Rose Productions Ltd., all rights reserved.

Parts of the manuscript were read by several of our colleagues who gave generously their time in order to give us feedback. Any errors that remain are ours alone. We want to thank Tony Burgess, Avril Loveless, Robert Mahon, Merciless Meg Maguire of Battersea, Peter Smagorinsky, Brian Street and Tom Are Trippestad in this regard.

Finally, we wish to thank our co-investigators on the Work of Teacher Education project – Allan Blake and Jim McNally from Strathclyde University. Not only did they enable us to complete a fairly ambitious but modestly funded project through their generosity and hard work but we learned a great deal from them in the course of conducting the research. We also had fun. Thank you, Allan and Jim.

Introduction: Transforming Teacher Education

PRIN [addressing final year student teachers]: Be extraordinary. Show them how to be extraordinary people. I am an extraordinary person. You are extraordinary people, because I say you are. There are not many of us. Not yet. Propagate your kind. Good luck.

DAVIES *(1989, p. 8)*

Written by the British screenwriter Andrew Davies, *Prin* tells the story of the principal of 'one of the last and best of the independent colleges of education' and her attempts to navigate a reorganization of teacher training at an unspecified point in the 1970s. Throughout this period, there had been increasing pressure from the policy sphere for a shift away from single-purpose training colleges and the Certificate (CertEd) and Bachelor of Education (BEd) routes into teaching towards a first degree in a subject followed by a Postgraduate Certificate of Education (PGCE). There had also been a major economic recession leading to significant cuts in the public services. At the same time, following the Robbins Report of 1963, there were profound changes in the organization of higher education in England (an overall expansion of the system and the creation of a new type of 'plate glass' [Beloff 1968] university) and the significant growth of a university-based infrastructure for educational research (Furlong 2013). The choice facing Prin was unappealing to her: merge with the local polytechnic and see her college's 'pursuit of excellence' become subsumed into what she sees as an inferior 'vocational' portfolio or become absorbed into the nearby 'third-rate' university where she would be offered a personal chair in what she nonetheless saw as a mundane parade of foundational disciplines 'plodding' through the motions of something she can barely bring herself to describe as 'research'.

Prin's view of the work of teacher preparation was distinctive. She took young women, sometimes 'mediocre...out of compassion', from lower middle- and working-class backgrounds and turned them into 'extraordinary' members of a new professional class whose lessons must be 'forms of life worth living for their own sake'. As students, they would of course take classes in the range of subjects necessary for them to be able to cover the primary school curriculum but the subjects themselves were not the point at all. The point was to enable a personal and professional transition for the select few across the lines of class and gender and to encourage their capacity to stimulate similar potential for social mobility among their own pupils, effected mainly on the basis of a putatively shared good taste. Prin's own subject expertise was in human movement and the philosophy of physical education and, although she made it clear she had written probably the most authoritative books on these topics, her specialist knowledge was not of the kind that could be easily written down. Her kind of knowledge was intangible, seductive and elusive; it stuck to some students and fell off others; it couldn't be planned for. The degree to which it stuck was the extent to which the student teacher pursued the college's overriding principle of 'excellence' and, as always for Prin, 'some are more excellent than others'.

The lecturers in the college were a mixed bunch and Prin didn't conceal her contempt for most of them. The worst offenders were the younger ones, those with ambitions to write a definitive book on this or that, ambitions Prin felt in her bones would never come to fruition. Others, like Dr Boyle, had PhDs and this marked them out as suspect from the start. They might have specialized in science education or children's literature and they may well have published occasional papers in their field's journals. But they did not have the same motivation as Prin; they did not share the same commitment to preparing 'extraordinary people' or organizing their work around 'the pursuit of excellence'. They had different aspirations and different fallibilities. Prin viewed most of them as lacking in originality and intelligence: neither one thing (a pursuer of excellence) nor the other (a true intellectual). They lacked her commitment to producing teachers who would 'bloom like terrifying exotic flowers in classrooms all over the country'; they certainly lacked her messianic fervour. At the end of the play, Prin stands down and Dr Boyle becomes interim principal as the college prepared to merge with the polytechnic. There were good opportunities on the horizon for the development of science education, according to Dr Boyle, and the career development of the teacher educators at the college too. Prin's era – the age of the single-purpose training college – was largely over.

The degree to which *Prin* captured some of the personal-institutional and professional-academic dynamics underlying a major reconfiguration of Initial Teacher Education (ITE) in England, should not come as a surprise. Andrew Davies, the author of the play, worked as a teacher educator at Coventry College of Education through its amalgamation with the

University of Warwick in 1978 until he left teacher education for a full-time writing career in 1987. Davies saw the College of Education become the university's Institute of Education and a national and international leader in ITE, continuing professional development and research, with strengths in literacy and English education, the arts and drama education (international creativity guru Ken Robinson worked there in the 1990s), religious education and several other areas. In 2013, however, by then an honorary professor at the university's School of Theatre, Performance and Cultural Policy Studies, Davies saw Warwick's Institute of Education closed to be replaced by a Centre for Education Studies (an academic unit housing master's and doctoral programmes and research) and the Centre for Professional Education (a 'business unit' and 'global service provider for high-quality training and professional education') [http://www2.warwick.ac.uk/fac/soc/cpe/]. Warwick had turned the page on that part of its history associated with the initial preparation of teachers within an academic environment. ITE had become market-sensitive, vocational service provision within a Russell Group university (one of the twenty-four most research-intensive universities in the UK).

Prin captured a particular historical moment in the history of higher education in England and in the organization of teacher education, specifically. Specialist single-purpose colleges grew up in the nineteenth century and early twentieth century to produce ever more teachers for the expanding population that had been given the right to elementary education. These colleges were, from one perspective, in the vanguard of an expanding system of higher education, granting Teacher's Certificates to pupil-teachers who met the standard after a 5-year practical apprenticeship and evening classes. Yet after the Second World War, they became subject to pressure from different sources – the urgent need for new teachers to address a post-war shortage in England and a new form of emergency training; the recommendations of the McNair Report (1944) and proposed regional arrangements with universities; the general expansion of higher education following the Robbins Report in 1963; the mergers and amalgamations of the 1970s; the increasing expectations of research activity for all those who pursued an academic career; the re-designation of most higher education institutions (HEIs) in England as universities by the Further and Higher Education Act of 1992 and the tight control of funding for ITE that differed from other forms of higher education funding (Crook 1997, Dent 1977, Furlong 2013, Gosden 1972). The rise of the pupil–teacher centres and day training colleges that became specialist colleges of education was stalled by the twin forces of profound change to the organization of – and expectations of – higher education overall and by changing understandings of what it meant to be a teacher, the kinds of knowledge and skills and expertise that were required to function effectively in schools that were themselves changing rapidly. 'Blooming like terrifying exotic flowers in classrooms' was no longer enough to qualify you as a teacher (if, indeed, it ever had been).

These sorts of complex and dynamic changes are not merely of nostalgic interest or processes we might look back on coolly from settled, higher ground. They are also part of the cultural–historical arena of teacher education as an activity of higher education today. Traces of practices and patterns of identity formation laid down over the last 100 years are still present in the ways of doing teacher education today. One of our own places of work, Brunel University, in the west of London, has its origins partly in the Borough Road College, founded as a teacher training institution in 1817, based on the earlier school set up by Joseph Lancaster in south-east London in 1798. Borough Road College moved west to Isleworth in 1890 and, with further amalgamations, became the West London Institute of Higher Education in 1976. The West London Institute became the Osterley campus of Brunel University through amalgamation in 1997 and eventually moved onto the main Brunel campus in the London Borough of Hillingdon in 2005. Yet, at the time of writing this book, there were still physical education teachers in London who described themselves as 'Borough Road teachers' and academic staff in Brunel's Department of Education who applied to work at the West London Institute. 'Borough Road teachers' were not part of the master's-level credit economy that has grown up in ITE in England in recent years. West London teacher educators did not necessarily sign up for a PhD and a career in a comprehensive, research-intensive university.

Brunel is not unusual. Far from it, similar situations have played out again and again around England as municipal day training colleges became colleges of education that merged, for example, with polytechnics that were granted the title of university. Our other place of work, Oxford University, has a strong tradition of ITE, yet the department in which it is based (the Department of Education) also had its origins in a day training college and a 'delegacy' initially outside of the collegiate university. In was only in the late twentieth century that both the department and its academic staff were gradually incorporated into the university itself. Indeed, until relatively recently, the majority of the academic staff of Oxford's Department of Education were former schoolteachers who had moved into higher education to teach on its once innovative Internship Scheme ITE programme (Benton 1990). So, for the whole range of HEIs in England, while new frames of reference and new trajectories of development became available for institutions and individuals alike, former ways of understanding the social world of teacher education remained and sometimes, unsurprisingly, clashed with the new. So the past has lived on in the present in the education of teachers through historically sedimented cultural practices, forms of identification and community, and trajectories of development that are already in process.

And that is our key interest in this book and in the research that underpins it. We are interested in how teacher education, specifically ITE, has come to be the way it is and how a different future might be possible. We begin from the premise that higher education's involvement in the preparation of teachers is a good idea that is borne out by the international research evidence. We do not seek to recapture the past or preserve the *status quo*. In looking at ITE in England and putting it into international context, we do not offer purely historical or sociological analyses of the current situation. Instead, driven by educational questions and interests, we attempt to analyse what goes on in the name of teacher education from the perspective of the higher education-based teacher educator – in England, the Lecturer in Education – the person appointed to an academic contract at an HEI with their main responsibility being the initial preparation of teachers. So we are interested in the field – teacher education – and regard the field as being made up of the labour of the academic practitioners in that field – the teacher educators – as they work together with students on their preparation as schoolteachers. We are interested in the *work* of teacher education. By focusing on the work, the labour of teacher educators and the social structures and material condition within which they are situated, we believe we gain some essential insights into how teachers are prepared and how they might be prepared better.

Our focus on the work of the higher education-based teacher educator is somewhat unusual in the literature and we make no apology for taking this approach. Our view is that for too long ITE has been seen as an activity that is separate from the rest of higher education, the problems and questions that have challenged the sector, the organization and funding of HEIs and the changing nature of academic work. Instead, we want to re-emphasize teacher education as an important form of higher education and to situate our exploration of ITE within larger questions about the organization and purposes of higher education. Our interest is in the transformation of teacher education as a form of higher education and to do that, we believe, a reconfiguration of the work of teacher education as academic work is required. The benefits of such a reconfiguration are potentially greater than for the individual teacher educator and the academic field of teacher education. The wider education system, schools, the teaching profession and young people all stand to gain from doing ITE differently.

The 'amazing challenge' of teacher education: What should teacher educators do?

Writing for the Organisation for Economic Co-operation and Development (OECD) in 2010, Pauline Musset provided a useful summary of the importance of teacher education for contemporary educational reformers:

> To design policies that... educate and train teachers, capable of helping students to acquire the competencies needed to evolve in today's societies and labour markets is an amazing challenge. In today's context, with the undergoing economic and social changes, high-quality schooling is more important than ever.... The debate on teacher education has gained special importance as teacher quality is more and more being identified as decisive to student outcomes. It is now acknowledged that teachers are the school variable that influences the most student achievement (OECD 2005). Education reforms that do not take into account teacher education are condemned to inefficiency (OECD 1998). (Musset 2010, p. 3)

Teacher education clearly has a central role in the improvement of educational systems around the world. When system outcomes are measured in economic terms and teachers and teaching are conceived of as variables, it is also clear that the concept of improvement is underpinned by a particular system of values. The efficient delivery of measurable gains against international benchmarks (such as the OECD's Programme for International Student Assessment – PISA) might appear to be the overarching goal. Whereas once teacher education's mission might have been to produce a new kind of professional (the schoolteacher) that would in turn produce a new kind of morally and ethically self-regulating person able to survive the risks of newly industrialized societies (Popkewitz 1998), now teacher education is seen by some as a form of emergency training for deliverers of human capital in advanced and aspiring knowledge economies.

Around the world, ITE continues to be in a state of almost continual reform, even crisis. Prin would recognize the dynamics if not the details. In some countries, traditional programmes of professional preparation in which universities are in leading roles are positioned as ineffective, unresponsive and incapable of producing the human capital required for economies to be globally competitive. In these countries and others, 'alternative' programmes of professional preparation have arisen and have become favourites of reform movements and governments alike. Teach for America, founded in 1990 by Wendy Kopp, was initially intended to train teachers for hard-to-staff schools in urban and rural areas in the United States – a form of emergency training, if you like. Over time, it has developed into a major international network – Teach for All (teachforall.org) – with thirty-two similar ITE projects funded by a mix of private philanthropic and state/public resources. In these new forms of teacher education, the role of higher education is different and is differently positioned in the rhetoric. Higher education is more marginal in the reformist alternatives than in the traditional programmes, although the actual situation is often more complex.

But the kind of teacher required by reform movements requires a different kind of preparation, generally speaking, and therefore a different kind of work on the part of the teacher educator in an HEI. This book takes forward the argument that what higher education teacher educators actually *do* therefore matters a great deal. The work of the teacher educator has an important relationship to the kind of teacher that is necessary for the system (on the system's terms). So although it is accepted that teacher education has a central role in educational reform and the improvement of school systems, what do the people who work in this academic field actually *do*? Day to day, how do they support the development of new teachers? What opportunities do they create for their learning – in schools and elsewhere? We believe that what teacher educators do – their work – matters. It matters in terms of the kind of teacher our schools need – to caricature the choice, either a professional or a missionary; it matters in terms of what these teachers learn to do – and how they do it; it matters, in the most basic sense, in terms of having enough teachers to staff schools and enough teachers who stay in the job long enough to become as effective as they might.

Governments and reformers know that what teacher educators do matters. That is why so many reform movements seek to remove teacher education from higher education altogether or, as in some recent developments in the United States, create alternative forms of HEI – 'graduate schools of education' with degree-awarding powers based on charter schools and charter school networks. The Relay Graduate School of Education in New York (http://www.relay.edu) and the Charlie Sposato Graduate School of Education in Massachusetts (http://www.matcheducation.org/match-teacher-residency/sposato-graduate-school-education) are two examples. What the teacher educators do in these programmes – their work – differs in degree from what teacher educators do in other universities and colleges in New York and Massachusetts. For Relay and the Sposato Graduate Schools, that is the selling point.

In England, former Education Secretary Michael Gove memorably termed an educational establishment that included higher education-based teacher educators 'the Blob', after the 1950s B-movie (Gove 2013), borrowing the language from former US Education Secretary William Bennett in the 1980s (Montague 1987). The Blob – teacher educators in universities, local education officials, trade unionists, unspecified others – all slow down politically driven education reforms. Indeed, one of Gove's former ministerial team, Nick Gibb, made the issue very explicit in an opinion piece he wrote for *The Guardian* newspaper entitled 'Teaching unions aren't the problem – universities are' (Gibb 2014). In response to the question 'who is to blame for our education system slipping down the international rankings?', Gibb wrote, 'the academics in the education faculties of our universities'. And just in case we think that the Conservative-Liberal Democrat coalition government in England held an usual opinion on this matter, it is worth remembering that it was under the previous Labour administration that Teach First (the English version of Teach for America) was established and expanded and that this critical suspicion of university Education departments was evident in the views of former Labour Education Minister Andrew Adonis (2012), whose thinking was so influential on Gove's personal agenda as Education Secretary (Gove 2012). So it is not only us who think that what teacher educators do – their work – matters.

The direction of this book

Given the context that we have started to sketch above, we think that the work of teacher educators as a policy and research problem requires urgent attention for two main reasons. First, the pace of reform in teacher education internationally – but perhaps especially in England and the United States – means that the scope and the scale of the changes are lost in a plethora of detail. The trajectory of reforms in recent years have *not* been to modify or revise the existing means of production of new teachers but have attempted to reconceive teachers and teaching and establish new regimes of governance and authority on entirely different terms to former understandings of professionalism. Second, while some teacher educators and researchers might critique the reforms and the reformers, the grounds for these arguments are often set by the reformers themselves and therefore often conservative, appearing to defend the *status quo*. In this book, we seek to break out of the reform/defend binary and to provide the ground for new arguments about transforming teacher education as a higher education activity so that it is of more benefit to the education system overall. We think it is important to look honestly and critically at what goes on in higher education in the name of ITE, figure out how it came to be so and how it might be reconfigured for the benefit of all stakeholders – schools, universities, policy-makers and the wider society.

The book has three aims:

1   To offer an account of the recent history and politics of teacher
    education, with particular reference to England but in an international
    context, paying attention to the policy but also the practices of
    teacher educators based in HEIs; we usually refer to England rather
    than the UK as a whole as political devolution among the four
    countries of the UK in the late 1990s built on some quite different
    historical cultures of education, especially in Scotland and Northern
    Ireland.

2   To show how the work of teacher educators and the practices of
    teacher education as a field afford and constrain different kinds of
    development for teachers, different types of and qualities of learning –
    and why this matters.

3   To suggest an agenda for the development of the field and its
    practitioners that might have wider benefits for the whole system and,
    although arising from our English context, have some international
    relevance.

These aims will be pursued through the six chapters that follow. In
Chapter 1, we continue our discussion of the current situation of
teacher education policy and practice in England, how this relates to
the international context and the evidence (such as it is) of what makes
effective teacher education programmes, with particular reference to the
United States and Finland. We look at changes in the identification of
teachers as professionals and changes in higher education as well as the
role of higher education in teacher preparation in school systems that are
deemed to be successful around the world.

In Chapter 2, we turn to an analysis of teacher education as a form of
higher education and also as a form of academic work. We draw on our
research into institutional conceptualizations of ITE as academic work that
involved analyses of job advertisements and job descriptions for teacher
educator positions as well as interviews with a small sample of heads (chairs)
of university Education departments, again putting our findings into the
context in the international research literature and a replication of our study
in Australia. Chapter 3 continues the discussion of our empirical research
into the work of teacher education by reporting on the 'Work of Teacher
Education' project, a mixed methods study of HEI-based teacher educators
over the course of a year. Again, the findings of our research are put into
context with research from other English-speaking countries in which teacher
education is seen as the domestic labour of university Education departments

subject to a gendered division of labour. We introduce the idea of 'academic capitalism' (Rhoades & Slaughter 1997, Slaughter & Leslie 1997) in relation to our discussions of what academics do and why.

Chapter 4 comprises four accounts of HEI-based teacher educators at work in England, presented as 'narratives of experience'. The teacher educators were all women and the narratives constructed using data generated by us with participants in the 'Work of Teacher Education' project over a 2-year period. The data generated from an ethnographic perspective are represented as narrative accounts of practice that illustrate key themes in our understanding of teacher educators' work. In Chapter 5, we draw out the larger consequences of this understanding of teacher educators and teacher education within higher education building on the previous four chapters. These consequences, we argue, are most keenly felt in the professional knowledge newly qualified teachers are able to draw on, their capacity to teach responsively and, ultimately, their retention within the profession. In the final chapter, Chapter 6, we draw on studies of teacher education, higher education pedagogy, sociocultural theories of learning and development, the sociology of science and of knowledge creation to suggest an agenda for the transformation of teacher education that, while arising out of the English context, might have relevance internationally. Our proposals may well mean radical change for the way we have done ITE in the past and shifts in responsibilities for schools and HEIs and the ways in which they see their roles in the education of teachers. But we are not arguing from either reformist position or defensive positions. We do not unquestioningly subscribe to an ideology of markets, competition and measurement of outcomes on purely economic terms. Neither do we argue that things should stay as they are, that what has gone on in the name of ITE has been wonderful and as good as it could ever be. Instead, we argue for a transformation of existing arrangements – roles, relationships, responsibilities, programme designs – that will lead to the development of the system. Ultimately, it is a pedagogical argument about the values that underpin this potential development, the ways in which the growth of the system can be stimulated and the kinds of teacher and teacher educator we would wish to see in ideal terms.

Transforming the object of activity: Our theoretical perspective in brief

In our research, we have not been motivated simply to reveal the extent to which current policy determines what teacher educators 'do' but to examine the complex relationships between individual agency and social structure in which culture and political economy have to be accounted for. Indeed, in aiming to examine the *work* of teacher educators, it is necessary to consider underlying economic values and social relations rather than seeing individual workers in isolation. Consequently, the design of our studies and our arguments in this book have been informed by cultural–historical activity theory (CHAT) (Cole 1996, Ellis et al. 2010, Engeström 1987), a set of practical and theoretical approaches to studying human development derived from the work of Lev Vygotsky (1978, 1986).

CHAT is premised on Marxian concepts and common interests in the relationships between culture, socially organized activity and human consciousness, and between value, commodities and labour. Marx's assertion that 'consciousness does not determine life; life determines consciousness' (Marx & Engels 1845–1846/1964, p. 37) became the basis for Vygotsky's materialist psychology and in turn influenced CHAT's interest in the social organization of human activity and the changes in consciousness it might be possible to stimulate within activity systems through interventions (c.f. Engeström 2007a). Understanding the social organization of the collective work of teacher education was our primary goal and the first stage in the arguments presented in this book. From this perspective, it was necessary to recognize work as embedded in specific social contexts and thus open to interpretation as a form of participation in these contexts (Reeves & Boreham 2006). Unlike CHAT-informed studies that focus more on understanding the psychological processes of the research participants, we have adopted a more materialist and grounded approach to the analysis of teacher educators' work, of the type advocated by Martin and Peim (2009).

In our researches, we wished to focus on what is sometimes known as the 'bottom line' of the Engeströmian triangular representation of human activity as a system: the *rules* for – or norms of – participation in cultural practices; the membership of the *community* held together and engaged by those practices and the *division of labour* among the members of that particular community (who gets to do what kind of work and why?). Division of labour, being a central concept in Marxian theory, was important to us in our analysis of teacher educators' work, both in HEI-based activity systems behind university walls and also in school–university partnerships or boundary zones where the work is divided up on the basis of historically evolved cultural norms between schoolteachers and HEI-based teacher educators. Although not in Engeström's tradition of Developmental Work Research (Engeström 2007a), we did nonetheless incorporate a participatory phase in the design of our 'Work of Teacher Education' study, funded by the UK Higher Education Academy. Unlike some CHAT-informed research, we have not felt compelled to insert triangular diagrammatic representations of our data in what follows. The triangle is intended for use as a mediating tool in formative interventions designed to help practitioners develop their practices and our studies have not been intervention studies in that sense.

It is worth dwelling for a moment on the concept of 'object' in CHAT and the related meaning of transformation. For Vygotsky's student Aleksei Leont'ev, the object of activity was actually its 'object-motive', which he explained as follows:

> The main thing which distinguishes one activity from another, however, is the difference in their objects. It is exactly the object of an activity that gives it a predetermined direction. According to the terminology I have proposed, the object of the activity is its true motive. (Leont'ev, 1978, p. 62)

The object of an activity is both what engages and motivates the participation of individuals in a collective activity. By initially perceiving a shared object and then by collectively working on it, the object is a cultural and historical phenomenon that is both fashioned and potentially transformed through the volitional participation of individuals. Working on the object involves encountering and negotiating contradictions, personally experienced but also structural constraints that need to be overcome and broken away from in order for new forms of the activity to emerge and for human agency to lead human development. Analysing these contradictions and negotiating new forms of collective activity might lead to reconfiguration of the social practices and the object of the activity. That is why learning and the creation of new knowledge, from an activity–theoretical perspective, is sometimes described as the transformation of the object of activity; it is a dialectical process that involves new ideas and new ways of organizing the work. Transformation, in CHAT terms, involves both a cultural–historical analysis and a future-oriented desire to produce new social arrangements that are simultaneously practical and intellectual. That expansive understanding of transformation – in which the terms of contradictory propositions are sublated – is the meaning of transformation we propose for teacher education in this book.

1

Teacher Education as a Policy Problem

In this chapter, we extend our discussion of the history and politics of teacher education reform and, in particular, examine how governments' and others' interests in teacher quality and teacher supply over the last 35 years have made ITE a public policy problem. This discussion helps us to show how policy interventions focused on the reconstruction of teachers and teaching have had a profound impact on HEI-based teacher educators' work. Combined with the sorts of changes to higher education we mentioned earlier and to which we return to in the following chapters, these policy trajectories have come together to position ITE awkwardly within higher education, especially in England where HEI-based teacher educators have strong lines of accountability within the school inspection system as well as statutory responsibilities to deliver school reforms to new teachers. That said, as we argue throughout the book, higher education has been and continues to be subject to its own reform and policy interventions and HEIs overall can be awkward places to sit.

Our discussion is mostly focused on England given that our research took place in this context and also because we believe England offers an interesting case internationally of a system that has some features of the market and other features of centralizing control derived from a historical welfare state. Later in the chapter, we also briefly refer to the United States and to Finland as they offer contrasting cases in terms of the analysis we are making about policy trajectories, higher education and the teaching profession. In the final section of the chapter, we review what is known about successful systems of ITE around the world, with a disclaimer that individual aspects of these systems cannot simply be ripped from their cultural and historical contexts to provide easy lessons for would-be reformers.

Linking education and economics: Teachers matter

Around the world, education systems are increasingly defined in terms of being able to 'respond to the twin revolutions of globalisation and the knowledge economy' (Giddens 2000, p. 162) by producing a suitably qualified and skilled workforce for the twenty-first century. The current British Prime Minister, David Cameron, has often been heard referring to the UK being 'in a global race' and in a speech to the Confederation of British Industry (CBI), he claimed that in order to participate effectively in this global race, his government had 'to be radical' and 'shake up' education (Cameron 2012). As Marilyn Cochran-Smith noted over 6 years ago (2008), the assumption that education and economic competitiveness are 'inextricably linked' (p. 271) is now prevalent amongst policy-makers in many nation states. Indeed, in the years since this observation was made, this neoliberal premise for policy-making has become so entrenched in ways of perceiving and understanding the world that it has become a form of educational common sense. Teachers can often be viewed as producers of 'human capital' – meaning, in this sense, the kinds of skills and capabilities required for economic productivity – and the values by which education is judged are therefore also economic.

It is worth spending a moment defining what we mean by neoliberalism and why it is both useful and not useful in our analysis. David Harvey (2005), anthropologist and expert reader of Marx, defines it as:

> in the first instance a theory of economic practices that proposed that human well-being can best be advanced by liberating individual entrepreneurial freedoms and skills within an institutional framework characterised by strong private property rights, free markets and free trade. (p. 2)

British sociologist of education Stephen Ball (2012) carefully distinguishes between the meaning of neoliberalism in terms of economic and of social relations and cautions that the word has been used so often that 'it is in danger of becoming meaningless' (p. 3). Indeed, in our reading of some recent sociology of education, teachers (whether in schools or in universities) often come across as being determined in their very being and in every activity by the ideological messages of the Mont Pelerin Society; it is a view of teachers that regards them as mere sock puppets of a neoliberal 'movement'. As Ball argues, though, neoliberalism is not so much a 'concrete economic doctrine' as an often contradictory set of economic and practices organized around the idea of the 'market'. In the end, neoliberalism 'is about both money and minds, and … is a nexus of common interest between various forms of contemporary capital and the contemporary state' (p. 3). Our own research has been motivated by an interest in how human agency and creativity (on the part of teacher educators, specifically) complicate the enactments of policies that might be termed either neoliberal or neoconservative and produce unexpected ruptures and dissonances. The link in the policy that Cochran-Smith described, between education and economic competitiveness, is nonetheless an entrenched and ubiquitous one in many countries.

The specific connections between teacher education, teacher supply and teacher quality, school output data and economic competitiveness were strongly emphasized by the OECD in its 2005 report *Teachers Matter*, a report that identified teacher quality as central in efforts to improve the quality of education (OECD 2005). Unsurprisingly then, politicians in many countries have continued to intervene in education systems in order to improve teacher supply and quality and inevitably teacher education – specifically pre-service or initial preparation (ITE) – has become an important lever of reform. Indeed, Furlong, Cochran-Smith and Brennan draw attention to how teacher education across the world is being conceived as a central public policy problem as 'teaching and teacher education are tightly linked to the nation's aspirations for global competitiveness' (Furlong et al. 2009a, p. 3). Reforms as 'solutions' to this policy problem can often be seen as mainly neoliberal in their values and intent as they not only are organized around a market principle (of purchasers and providers) but around a new idea of the role of the state and a way of governance (Ball 2012).

The problem of the 'new teacher education'

Cochran-Smith, in her presidential address to the American Educational Research Association (AERA) in 2004, described how concerns in the United States surrounding teacher supply and teacher quality in the late 1990s had led policy-makers to focus upon teacher preparation – from this point ITE became a 'public policy problem'. A consequence of this policy turn has been that governments of all persuasions have come to believe that the 'quality of its teachers depends on the quality of its policies' (Cochran-Smith 2008, p. 277). In many respects, it is a naïve view of policy and one that politicians are usually disabused of after a term in office. Nonetheless, emerging out of this 'policy turn' is the 'new teacher education', which according to Cochran-Smith has three interlinked aspects: 'it is constructed as a public policy problem, based on research and evidence, and driven by outcomes' (Cochran-Smith 2009, p. 11). In other words, while there is sometimes a commitment to 'the implementation of research-based policies regarding teacher education [that] will solve the teacher supply problem and enhance teacher quality, thus leading to increased pupil achievements', the nature of the research and the validity of the evidence are often highly contested (Cochran-Smith 2008, p. 273).

As is the case with most policy areas in the United States, the new teacher education is constructed by both neoliberal and neoconservative discourses. Neoliberalism, as we have said, promotes market approaches and creates competition within a sector (among 'providers' of ITE, for example) with the aim of improving the quality of delivery of outcomes (which even though tied to the person and their well-being are often measured in solely economic terms). Neoconservative thinking, on the other hand, with its 'strong central cultural authority' (Apple 2001, p. 182) champions the standards movement and canonical approaches to knowledge and, often, systems of national accreditation. Under such a complex regime – a system of 'free markets and increased surveillance' (Apple 2001, p. 190) – rather than there being research into what works for the good in teacher education, there has been a proliferation of elaborate assessment systems preoccupied with gathering evidence – often in its narrowest form – about student teacher outcomes. This narrow version of evidence, Cochran-Smith (2009) warns us, can tell us little about the bigger educational questions, for example, how to meet the needs of an increasingly diverse pupil population. Nor can it shed light onto issues relating to questions about values and priorities; after all these cannot be answered by evidence alone. Furthermore, in the new teacher education there are attempts to directly link teacher quality with pupil outcomes where pupil outcomes are most often judged by performance on standardized tests alone.

There are, however, inherent dangers in doing things this way. When such a narrow version of pupil outcomes is relied upon to judge both teacher quality and by implication 'to police the results of teacher education' (Apple 2001, p. 188), there is insufficient regard given to the inherent complexity in the system and the social and cultural differences that exist more widely. Therefore, the new teacher education, with its 'narrow version of evidence-based practice' (Cochran-Smith 2009, p. 13), is unlikely to provide any insights into the most effective ways to educate the increasingly diverse pupil populations across a globalizing world. Moreover, in failing to acknowledge difference and inequality, the new teacher education will do little to meet the needs of the next generation of citizens capable of functioning in a democratic world where knowledge, skills and dispositions are ranging and far outside of what is testable (see Darling-Hammond 2006, Zeichner & Sandoval 2013).

More recently, reformers claim that there have been attempts to connect initial teacher preparation and their continuing professional development to 'meeting the needs' of diverse student populations. The 'needs' in question, however, are again usually interpreted as increased test scores and progression through the education system in order to become better prepared for the world of work and to improve the national economy's global competitiveness. The phrase 'narrowing the gap' has become associated with this sort of approach, founded on the assumption that specific teaching practices are universally more effective than others in raising attainment and also founded on the assumption that the attainment of those at the top of the tree (above the gap) will remain static. In England, the phrase became part of the framework for the school inspection system (Ofsted 2007) and in the United States has been used in some more neoconservative solutions for raising standards by teaching 'core' knowledge to all (Hirsch 2013).

Teacher education reform policies in the international context

In this section, we first take a close look at the recent historical development of policy for teacher education in England in order to set the ground for the two chapters that follow and the discussion of our research into teacher education as academic work. We then look briefly at the United States and at Finland as contrasting examples where policy trajectories and institutional and professional cultures are very different and conclude with a section that attempts to summarize what it is we do know about ITE in 'effective' education systems around the world.

England

Although occasionally seen as 'something of a backwater' politically (Furlong et al. 2000, p. 1), teacher education became a public policy problem in England in the early 1980s. Under Margaret Thatcher's Conservative government (1979–1997) there began a crucial period of reform for ITE, which at that time was solely situated in and led by higher education – in universities, polytechnics and colleges of education. It was during this period that political criticism of HEI-based teacher education with its 'jargon-ridden theorizing' (Keith Joseph, Conservative Secretary of State for Education, 1982, cited in Edwards et al. 2002, p. 60) intensified and its promulgation of supposedly 'left wing' liberal views held responsible for poor educational outcomes. The government's response was to make ITE a public policy problem and therefore in need of reform in order to loosen the stranglehold of higher education and so ensuring that the education and training of teachers were more responsive to political control (Iven 1994). Research by the Modes of Teacher Education (MOTE) team (Furlong 1996, Furlong et al. 2000) demonstrated that government reforms – beginning in 1984 with Circular 3/84 (DES 1984) – had changed the face of ITE in England dramatically in just 15 years. The MOTE study showed how the cumulative effect of the various policies had led to 'the invention of new routes into teaching that specifically excluded higher education, the definition of competences, the prescription of how (university-school) partnerships were to be formed, the undermining of the financial stability of schools of education in universities and colleges' – all of which had 'contributed progressively to curtail the influence of those in higher education on the professional development of new teachers' (Furlong et al. 2000, p. 143). Not only did HEIs lose financial control, from this point, the funding of ITE was separated from the general higher education funding streams, something that has continued to this day and has been increasingly used as a crude lever of government control.

Statutory partnerships between HEIs and schools were key to the reform movement: student teachers were to spend more of their time in school and schools were to be involved in the planning and organization of programmes. Indeed the rhetoric called for university–school partnerships to be more collaborative. However, as the MOTE study showed, in fact they largely remained university-led with little effective collaboration going on (Furlong et al. 2000). In fact, it seemed that the financial constraints caused by the routing of money away from universities and into schools had reduced the capacity for HEI-based teacher educators to work collaboratively with school colleagues. Furthermore, as HEIs took responsibility (and the reputational risks) for the outcomes of the regular inspections carried out by Her Majesty's Inspectors (HMI; later to become the Office for Standards in Education, Ofsted), many HEI staff took on more quality assurance work rather than a traditionally understood academic job. As Furlong et al. (2000) remind us, universities and colleges 'developed an increasingly practical orientation with relationships between those in schools and higher education narrowed to bureaucratic rather than collaborative relationships' (p. 165). This diminution of the specifically higher education contribution to the initial preparation of teachers has been a trend for around 30 years in England.

In his recent book, Furlong (2013) acknowledges that the years of Conservatism had been critical for teacher education in England, not least because the Conservatives' aim to marginalize HEI-based teacher educators had been achieved but also because 'any semblance of university autonomy evaporated without trace' (p. 37). Indeed, the degree to which HEIs appeared to cede responsibility and allow themselves to become subject to invasive and punitive inspections by Ofsted and volatile funding regimes was, in retrospect, startling and set precedents for much that has followed. Even a change of government in 1997 and the election of New Labour and Tony Blair as Prime Minister did nothing to rectify the situation as the policy trajectory instigated by the previous Conservative administration continued under New Labour, overlaid by its distinctive modernization agenda.

However, as was the case with the previous administration, New Labour's education policy agenda could be understood as a strongly neoliberal one (as suggested by the insertion of 'New' before 'Labour'). However, it seems that being faced with the complex system that had developed under the Conservatives, New Labour's response was to establish a more 'active state' (see Giddens 2000) so as to influence and police the education system more effectively. For New Labour, the main objective for teacher education was to produce teachers willing and able to adopt centrally defined government policies and targets that it deemed would raise standards and lead to increased economic competitiveness (Furlong 2013). Huge investment in the education system under New Labour led to changes not only in teachers' career structures and to pay rises but also to increasingly hard-line specification of what teachers should teach, when and how, by reforms such as the National Strategies (see Ellis 2011a).

While it is probably true to say that, unlike the Conservative government, New Labour did not explicitly seek to remove universities from teacher education, its policies actually did very little to re-establish or re-think the role of higher education in the preparation of new teachers nor did they reassert any autonomy. As before, partnership continued to be the central and defining feature of ITE and the promotion of more effective collaborative partnerships through the National Partnership Project (NPP) at one time became a government priority. However, in reality, rather than reducing allegiance to markets and competition, NPP proved to be little more than a short-term response to increase teacher supply (Furlong et al. 2009b). Under New Labour the nature of university–school ITE partnerships remained largely unaltered. As before, the relationships between teacher educators and their school colleagues often remained narrow and bureaucratic and were rarely collaborative. Given that under New Labour there had been substantial investment in education, including ITE, the failure of university leaders to support – philosophically and financially – true collaborative partnerships was a real missed opportunity. Rather than reducing the role of higher education, collaborative partnerships might actually have increased its role, as Furlong (1996) had suggested, by providing 'opportunities for higher education institution tutors to work with teachers on a regular and sustained basis, the chances of teacher educators increasing their influence on the profession are enhanced rather than reduced' (p. 53).

In contrast to the Conservatives, New Labour did not generally seem to question the role of higher education in ITE. Rather than being under siege and marginalized as it had been under the Conservatives, the future for higher education in ITE seemed to be more secure. However, this security came with a price: under New Labour, with its centralist tendencies and overt managerialism, the political and institutional interventionism actually intensified. The success of this level of intervention could be seen in the way in which it became possible for national policies for schooling to 'reach down into the detail of the day – today practice in teacher education programmes across the whole country' (Furlong et al. 2009a, p. 4). With specific reference to ITE, New Labour introduced a National Curriculum for Initial Teacher Training (DfEE 1997, 1998) that all 'providers' of ITE (to use the term that gained in currency during this period) were expected to follow, their compliance inspected by Ofsted. Teacher educators were obliged to teach to and assess against national standards and also to check their students' subject knowledge against nationally specified lists of content, oddly rather a neoconservative idea (see Ellis 2007). Again, in retrospect, it is remarkable that university leaders did not challenge such directive interventions on the grounds of academic freedom.

Although using the HEIs to deliver their schools' policy agenda on a statutory basis (universities were legally obliged to comply with the National Strategies, for example, whereas for schools they were technically only 'recommended'), New Labour also encouraged some diversity in the sector by introducing further 'alternative routes', such as the Graduate Teacher Programme (GTP) (for older graduates and career-changers with some relevant experience) and Teach First (the English version of Teach for America), principally to improve teacher supply. However, this diversification led to a further opening up of the teacher education market. Some have argued that it has been two factors – this diversity of provision and the existence of a culture of compliance and performativity within HEIs – that have served only to further weaken the position of higher education (Menter et al. 2006). Furthermore, the combination of prescribing standards together with the creation of a range of providers in maintaining a market has worryingly 'hollowed out' the contribution of higher education (Furlong 2013, p. 183). Furlong, perhaps overstating the situation in its generality, nonetheless argues that higher education's contribution had been hollowed out to such an extent that research, theory, critique were 'well and truly expunged as important components of professional education' (Furlong 2009, p. 55).

Despite this, there was little resistance to New Labour's policies from within higher education. Possibly there was no longer the fear that the Conservative's ambition to 'sever the connection' between the study of education in the university and its practice in schools would be achieved (Maclure 1993, p. 6 cited in Whitty et al. 2007, p. 10). Or perhaps it was that New Labour's continual interference had resulted in 'reform fatigue' (Seddon et al. 2013, p. 6) and this had created inertia in higher education and the hope that 'it would all go away'. Perhaps higher education leaders, like others, were seduced by the neoliberal rhetoric of social justice and thought that the market principle and the techniques of New Public Management would, in the end, actually 'narrow the gap' and improve social mobility. Or, more tactically and as part of the wider *realpolitik* of higher education, senior managers had decided to give away some control of ITE and the academics that did this work in the hope that the Elysian fields of educational research would be left unsullied and the questions asked of research quality and research funding would not be too pressing or too urgent.

Whatever the reasons might be, it seems that to some extent an uneasy peace broke out under New Labour. This peace was not without its problems. The political interventionism that occurred seems to have inculcated within HEI Education departments in England a culture of compliance, a culture in which teacher education has often (although fortunately not always) become defined in narrow and technical terms and certainly one in which HEIs perceive their agency in the professional education of new teachers as being quite dramatically limited (McNicholl et al. 2013).

The peace was also only a temporary truce. The Conservative-Liberal Democrat Coalition Government elected in May 2010 once again sought to marginalize higher education in the preparation of new teachers (even though the first Secretary of State for Education, Michael Gove, was occasionally heard to utter modest praise for those 'outstanding' universities that supported him). In the Coalition's White Paper *The Importance of Teaching* (DfE 2010) and subsequent policy papers (e.g. DfE 2011a, 2011b), it became clear that the justification for the Coalition's policy agenda is grounded in ideologies that champion traditional, even neoconservative notions of canonical knowledge, notions that invariably reduce teaching to little more than the transmission of this knowledge. Nick Gibb, a Coalition Schools' minister, articulated this view when he was reported stating that he would 'rather have a graduate from Oxbridge without a PGCE teaching in a school than a physics graduate from one of the rubbish universities with a PGCE' (Gibb 2010, np). The prominence given to teachers' subject knowledge rather than pedagogy now strongly defined excellent teaching for the Coalition. By implication, pedagogy was just something you picked up on the job, from 'experience' and by 'doing' (see Ellis & Orchard 2014). Teacher education lacked scientific knowledge and teaching was better understood as a craft.

The broader Coalition education policy agenda has seen the introduction of Free Schools and more Academies (a New Labour idea) – outside of local democratic structures and under contract directly to the Education

Secretary – and these schools were given 'freedoms' that included the right to employ unqualified teachers. Good graduates would do. Furthermore, schools were expected to have an increased role in ITE. To this end there has been an expansion of Teach First and the introduction of another school-based route called School Direct. Initially, School Direct posed a very real threat to the future of higher education's involvement in ITE as the 'core allocation' of places to HEIs made by the government's National College for Teaching and Leadership (NCTL) was reduced as the proportion of School Direct places (and funding) increased. With School Direct, schools were given the same technical status as a 'provider' of ITE and, in theory, selected their own student teachers and were expected to take responsibility for their training. In order to achieve this goal, the funding for each School Direct place is now being routed through schools. In practice, however, with schools lacking certain pieces of essential infrastructure such as specialist staff to process applications, handle compliance issues and also take responsibility for the quality of training in a high-risk, Ofsted-inspected environment, schools with School Direct places have channelled significant proportions of the funding back to HEIs to take on admissions, quality assurance and training functions. So although superficially it looks as though significantly more teachers are being prepared in schools through School Direct, on closer examination these teachers are still being trained in partnership with HEIs and coming into contact with other student teachers on those HEI's PGCE courses. HEIs are still involved and Coalition policy has not led to the end of higher education's contribution to the initial preparation of teachers. Early reports suggest that it is the quality and impact of what is going on under the name of a higher education contribution to School Direct that may now be the issue.

The trajectory of policy change and reform we have outlined in this section gives rise to the questions we have been posing about what HEI-based teacher educators do, how their work contributes to the development of new teachers. Before we move on to a closer examination of how HEIs in England have conceptualized and argued about teacher education as academic work in the public sphere, we turn briefly to two other countries that present interesting cases of higher education involvement in ITE, the United States and Finland. The United States is often held up as an example of an unsuccessful school system, one resistant to reform and doomed to fail its population of young people – even though distinguished educational psychologist David Berliner has recently used a fine statistical analysis to demonstrate that the effects of inequality and child poverty on student attainment are greater than those of teachers and schools (Berliner 2014). Finland, on the other hand, is usually held up as an example of a successful school system *par excellence* with high standards (including those represented in PISA) and high status for teachers – even though what happens in Finnish ITE programmes would be *anathema* to most UK and US teacher education reformers.

The United States

In contrast to the English situation, the recent history of teacher education policy in the United States is not a story of national policy-making. The Federal Government, given the US Constitution's Tenth Amendment, has a complex relationship with individual states that are each regarded as independent jurisdictions as far as education policy is concerned. This complexity does not mean that the Federal Government is without influence but it does not channel core funding for schools or set out the detail of policy, for either higher education or schools in the same way as in England. Given the longer history of mass higher education in the United States than in England and the more genuine market for higher education through a fee economy that also has a long history, the organization and funding of HEIs are also considerably different (Bok 2013, Clifford & Guthrie 1988, Labaree 2004, Pickard 2014).

That said, there has been a growth of influence of the Federal Government on state and local policies over time. The presidency of George W. Bush saw the passing of the *No Child Left Behind* Act in 2001 that promoted 'standards-based' educational reforms. The Obama administration has tried to exert more influence over national education policy through the implementation of the 2009 American Recovery and Reinvestment Act (ARRA) that has funded initiatives such as 'Race to the Top' and 'School Improvement Grants' and also in the appointment of former Chicago public schools chief executive Arne Duncan as federal Secretary of Education. Duncan had tried out several radical ideas with schools deemed poorly performing in that city and had sought to break out of local structures of political control and accountability and instead partnered with a variety of philanthropic organizations committed to systemic change. As Secretary of Education, Duncan authored the 2011 report *Our Future, Our Teachers* (Duncan 2011) that proposed additional grant funding for states that embraced certain reform ideas such as linking school-level value-added data to graduates of specific ITE programmes. Nationally, however, the Federal Government continues to operate within constitutional limits and can mainly seek to exert its influence through the provision of additional funds to states and local organizations that are prepared to meet federal criteria and be subject to federal evaluation.

ITE is also more visibly professionalized within US higher education career structures than is the case in England, on the basis of HEI statistical data (Furlong 2013, HESA 2009, Tierney 2001). Workers on career-grade academic contracts at US HEIs (whether or not those universities or colleges are regarded as research intensive or not) will be on the 'tenure track', meaning that they will have a doctoral degree, some evidence of capacity for research and the academic title of assistant professor (with opportunities for promotion to associate and then full professor and a right to permanent employment). The United States also has a strong professional community concerned with teaching and teacher education including organizations such as the American Association of Colleges of Teacher Education (AACTE) with its own conferences and scholarly publications as well as more policy-oriented professional bodies such as the National Board for Professional Teaching Standards (NBPTS) and the National Council for Accreditation of Teacher Education (NCATE), a voluntary, profession-regulated scheme.

Within this very different context, there has been perhaps a more complex reform tradition driven not only by federal initiatives but by individual states' agendas, the market for higher education, the interests of academic researchers and professional bodies and the strong culture of philanthropy that is increasingly associated with aspects of public policy in the United States (Saltman 2010). Indeed, as Cochran-Smith (2008) noted, the 'new teacher education' is characterized by some diversity of provision that includes the HEI-led programmes (sometimes referred to as 'college recommending') – through which the majority of US teachers continue to be prepared – and various 'alternatives', one of the most famous of which is Teach for America. Teach for America, as we have already noted, was founded by Wendy Kopp in 1989, intended in part to help address teacher shortages in urban and rural schools. It receives funding from federal and state taxation (often on a non-competitive basis) as well as from philanthropic endowments such as the Bill and Melinda Gates Foundation, the Eli and Edythe Broad Foundation and the Walton Family Foundation (heirs to the Walmart retail business).

A more recent initiative has been the development of Urban Teacher Residencies (UTRs), designed to prepare teachers for hard-to-staff urban school districts and to address teacher retention problems in those districts. UTRs have been promoted by the Federal Government through the ARRA as a means of improving teacher quality and teacher supply for schools deemed to be poorly performing (according to test scores), beginning with $43 million in 2009. UTRs share common characteristics such as a commitment to work-based learning (hence the idea of student teacher as 'resident' and programme as 'residency'), a strong partnership with schools in a school district, a commitment to raising standards of attainment in that district and a related commitment to improving teacher recruitment and retention in the schools. Usually, they are operated in association with an HEI and lead to a master's degree and a teaching credential. Residents also usually receive a stipend and pay reduced tuition fees for their degree from funding that is made available by both Federal Government and philanthropic interests. The rise of the UTR is a good example of the ways in which the Federal Government can influence and stimulate developments in teacher education by making funds available for preferred initiatives (that states and local education organizations can opt into if they choose) and also of the way in which recent federal policy directions align with those often described, after Saltman (2010), as 'venture philanthropists'.

Zeichner and Sandoval (2013) noted how this group of philanthropists have used their private capital to establish rules of public policy:

> Specifically, the entrepreneurial community has been able to establish the criterion for judging the quality of a teacher education programme based on how many of its graduates are able to raise students' standardised test scores at a given moment in time. Questions about the costs in doing so (e.g. stripping down the curriculum), how long these graduates stay in teaching, and how well they are able to support student learning in a broader sense beyond test scores do not get raised and discussed. (p. 8)

The convergence of the interests of private capital and the funding stimulus of the Federal Government is a notable feature of the current US policy context for teacher education. It is also worth noting, however, that in the two examples of reform ideas we have discussed in this section (Teach for America and UTRs), HEIs are still involved to the extent of providing training programmes and academic accreditation. The Teach for America summer schools and other aspects of the programme are often provided in collaboration with universities who bid for a contract (in the same way as English HEIs are an essential part of the Teach First programme). UTRs also involve partnerships between school districts and local universities who provide summer schools, evening classes and coursework and academic accreditation at master's level. The nature of UTRs, the kinds of partnerships they forge with HEIs and the quality and standards of the academic component can vary considerably, though, once again reminding us that it is not just the involvement of HEIs and higher education-based teacher educators that is important but what they do and the nature of their contribution to the process of learning to teach.

In 1990, Zeichner and Liston identified four historical traditions in teacher education reform in the United States. The first tradition was what they referred to as the 'academic tradition' where subject matter preparation was given the highest priority and pedagogical knowledge either devalued or ridiculed. The second was the 'social efficiency tradition' with its 'faith in the power of science' to provide a solid basis for a teacher education curriculum (p. 7). Third was the 'developmentalist tradition' with its origins in the study of child development, loosely termed 'progressive' and with interests in age- or developmental-stage-appropriate pedagogy. The fourth and final tradition they described as the 'social reconstructionist tradition', more explicitly political, often termed 'radical' and a more social just society as its goal. Recent teacher education reforms in the United States can perhaps be mapped most appropriately against the first two – the academic and the social efficiency traditions. Subject matter preparation is seen as vital and the quality of the prospective teachers' subject matter background (measured by proxies such as undergraduate coursework and standardized tests). Teaching, from the perspective of recent reforms, is often understood as a repertoire of discrete teaching routines that are deemed universally effective –on the basis of either the observations of a 'master teacher' (e.g. Doug Lemov's *Teach Like a Champion* (2010)) or the measurement of effect size in studies that claim to use experimental techniques. In both traditions, knowledge is just 'out there', to be handed down to student teachers just as it is to be transmitted to students in schools.

Finland

A small country of around 5.4 million people, Finland is often regarded as having the most successful education system outside Asia. As Reijo Miettinen (2013) points out, Finland's success is neither one of overnight success nor one of consistently high-level achievements over many decades. Miettinen traces the rise of Finland's education system over the last 15 to 20 years against a background of a wider programme of national, societal development after the Second World War and a period of more rapid changes in the 1960s that saw an economic transformation from an agrarian economy to an urban, industrial one. Comprehensive reforms of the school system were needed at the time in order to prepare new kinds of citizens needed for the new Finnish society.

As Miettinen also points out, the values underpinning this major shift in society and schooling were not neoliberal in the sense we have come to understand neoliberalism nor were they driven by a theory of 'human capital':

> ... the concept of human capital does not discuss the qualitative differences between education systems. It has difficulties in dealing with the capabilities most needed in the invention of new realities, namely critical thought, creativity and imagination. (p. 8)

What was planned for in Finland, in Miettinen's analysis, was a 'virtuous cycle' between building a national culture of innovation and developing a modern welfare state. The economic benefits of innovation fed back into the education, health and welfare systems and created the conditions for further innovation, driven by investment in the development of human capabilities such as creativity and criticality. (This was an analysis first made by Castells and Himanen in 2002 when trying to identify a 'Finnish model' of success in innovation.)

Changes to the ways in which teachers were prepared did not take place until 1971 when all ITE had to be provided at a university and also at master's level (Miettinen 2013, p. 109). However, it wasn't until the 1990s that teachers who had been through this new form of teacher education became the majority of the teaching workforce and it wasn't until 2000 that PISA began to make their comparative assessments. For policy-makers in other OECD countries, in particular those looking for quick solutions, it is probably inconvenient that Finland's success is likely to be an effect of a long-term strategy and doubly inconvenient that it is part of strategy that links developing a national culture of economic innovation with building a modern welfare state, in a 'virtuous cycle'.

Finnish teacher education researcher Hannele Niemi also draws our attention to the cultural and educational contexts in which teachers have been prepared:

> Many people ask why Finnish students perform so well in school and many young Finns choose teaching as their life career. There is no regular standardised testing, school inspection, teacher evaluation or ranking of schools in Finland. Public education has a central role in enhancing equality and well-being in Finnish society. High quality academic teacher education ensures readiness to work in other areas of the Finnish labour market. Most importantly, in Finland teachers and schools enjoy strong public confidence. Parents trust teachers the way they trust their dentists.... I believe that because teachers – as a result of academic education – have clear moral purpose and independent professional ethos, they are trusted. Research-based teacher education is essential in making that possible. (Niemi; cited in Sahlberg 2011, p. 84)

Picking up on Niemi's distinction, Pasi Sahlberg defines the overall system of teacher education in Finland as both 'academic' and 'research based'. The design and content of university-based master's courses for prospective teachers are based on these principles rather than on a system of national standards or ITE national curricula or monitoring inspections tied to funding or even 'nudges' in certain policy directions by government financial incentives, as in the United States. 'Academic teacher education' is defined by Sahlberg as 'based on and supported by scientific knowledge and ... focused on thinking processes and cognitive skills needed to design and construct educational research' (Sahlberg 2011, p. 78). 'Research-based teacher education' means:

> systematic integration of scientific educational knowledge, didactics (or pedagogical content knowledge), and practice to enable teachers to enhance their pedagogical thinking, evidence-based decision making, and engagement in the professional community of educators. (Sahlberg 2011, p. 78)

Both Niemi and Sahlberg acknowledge that there is a historically accumulated 'Finnish advantage' that may affect the country's performance in international league tables. Two aspects of this advantage are, first, that teaching within the Finnish culture is one of the highest status occupations and therefore applications to teacher education programmes are highly competitive. Second, teachers' salaries are slightly above the national average salary with progression up a more generous salary scale than, for example, in the United States; upper secondary school teachers in Finland can see a 78 per cent increase in their salary over the first 15 years (Sahlberg 2011, p. 77), and none of the salary is merit- or performance-based.

However, they also both identify what they believe is the most important condition for the Finnish education system's success: its concept of the teacher as a professional and teaching as professional work. Finland's success, in their view, is related to the capacity of the profession of teaching to allow teachers to 'fulfill their moral missions' (Sahlberg 2011, p. 76) and participate in a professional community of educators where the development of practice is built into the day-to-day expectations of the job of teaching and the balance of duties. As Sahlberg notes, in many countries the concept of a 'professional learning community' is one applied to arrangements that are contrived for teachers' professional development or in-service training, often in their own time. In Finland, 'schools are regarded as professional learning communities due to the inherent nature and balance of teachers' daily professional work' (Sahlberg 2011, p. 76).

As Toom et al. (2010) point out, however, the academic and research-based principles of Finnish teacher education are not intended to:

> educate researchers or even teacher-researchers *per se*. The objective is to acquire an inquiring attitude to teaching. Thus teachers are able to observe, analyse and develop their work. (p. 339)

In order to help prospective teachers and serving teachers meet this objective, teacher education is unproblematically a part of Finnish higher education and, indeed, it is deemed necessary for it to be a higher education activity in order for it to be at the right conceptual level and more open to wide, public scrutiny. However, when Viv Ellis spoke to some higher education-based teacher educators during site visits to Finland in 2012 and 2013, he found that there was sometimes a feeling that Finnish teacher education was somewhat 'traditional' in the sense that it hadn't changed or developed much in the last 20 years. And quite unlike England, for example, there is no minimum requirement for the amount of time (e.g. the number of weeks) a student teacher must spend in schools on placement, so there is some variation between the various universities' programmes. Once again, the trust and confidence placed in the national education system and the ways of preparing teachers for Finland's schools mean that such questions about the details of the design and content of programmes have not become a public policy problem as they have elsewhere in the world.

The previous sections have highlighted not only differences in the ways in which ITE in these countries is organized, funded and developed, they have highlighted major differences in political economy and national governance as well as differences in how teachers are understood as an occupational group. These major ideological and structural differences make it almost impossible to isolate 'variables' that may be significant in any direction. What the experience of these countries does show, however – even in such a complex, highly politicized and strongly market-driven context such as the United States – is that higher education continues to make a contribution to the initial preparation of teachers even when 'alternatives' to 'college-recommending' programmes are sought and, indeed, preferred.

In preparing teachers, do we know 'what works'?

The question of 'what works?' in teaching and in teacher education is a persistent question in many traditions of research and of policy development and, in some important ways, is a reasonable one given that teaching is an important activity that has both responsibilities and authority in society and it is also one that is in large part funded through general taxation. Teachers and teacher educators, like many other public sector professionals, are required to open up their practices for public scrutiny far more than they once were and public (or state) education is one of those areas of our lives as citizens in which we all have a right to contribute to the debate (see Chapter 5 for further discussion on this topic).

What we do know is that even in contexts where politicians have sought to marginalize or exclude higher education from ITE, HEIs are still involved in, for example, running summer schools and mentor training for Teach First in England or providing sometimes rigorous academic coursework and master's-level accreditation for UTRs in the United States. In those school systems that do well in international comparisons such as PISA, we also know that the OECD (2011a & b) has shown that a close focus on the practicalities of teaching in classrooms is combined with 'the opportunity to study how young people learn and to engage with findings of the latest pedagogical research [and] develop as researchers themselves with well supported opportunities to undertake Master's and doctorates' (Furlong 2014, p. 1). Even in balanced accounts of ITE across international contexts, the 'strong emphasis on using research based on state-of-the-art practice' and opportunities to 'pilot innovative practices and undertake research on learning and teaching' associated with the higher education contribution to ITE (OECD 2011a, p. 10) are identified among countries that are seen as the 'strongest performers' internationally. In these countries' systems, higher education takes part of the responsibility for 'preparing teachers to lead improvement' (OECD 2011a, p. 11) at the system level, by developing their capacity to undertake action research or participate in collaborative forms of professional development such as lesson study. In the case of Finland, building a strong, academic and research-based teacher education is seen as part of the 'virtuous cycle' of developing human capabilities within the welfare state and stimulating a culture of economic innovation.

Highly successful school systems around the world rely on higher education to contribute to the preparation of their highly successful teachers and also to their systems. Even countries that do not think their systems are highly successful tend to rely on HEIs to prepare the bulk of their new teaching workforce, even through alternatives to mainstream routes such as Teach First, UTRs or, as recently in England, School Direct. We also know that removing higher education altogether from teacher preparation or even removing the requirement for teachers to be qualified at all would likely have negative effects on the performance of the students they teach, regardless of how long those teachers have been teaching, according to a comprehensive statistical analysis of 7 years of student-level data from the city of Houston, Texas, by Stanford University researchers (Darling-Hammond et al. 2005). So the question, it seems to us, is not whether higher education should be involved at all in ITE but *how* it should be involved. That seems to us the more genuine question – and the more important one. And it is a question that has at its core debates about what HEI-based teacher educators should do, what kind of work is involved in the higher education contribution to the initial preparation of teachers, as well as how we understand teachers as an occupational group and how we understand teaching as professional work.

Concluding comments

In this chapter, we have looked at the recent teacher education policy trajectories in England and, to a lesser extent, in the United States and Finland. In each of these countries, we find HEIs involved in ITE, even in reforms of systems that would, on the surface, seek to marginalize or exclude them. In highly successful education systems such as those of Finland (and elsewhere) we find higher education an unproblematic part of the overall system with that is able to reach beyond the preparation of individual teachers into system-level improvement. The question that is raised by the evidence is not whether higher education should be involved in ITE but how it should be involved.

In the next chapter, we return specifically to the English context and our research into how HEIs conceptualize the work of teacher education and about how they argue in the public sphere about the work of HEI-based teacher educators when they seek to recruit them.

2

Teacher Education as Academic Work

In this chapter, drawing on a small-scale empirical study and a review of the literature, we examine how the HEI-based teacher educator is conceptualized as a category of academic worker at the institutional level in England. As in the rest of this book, by 'teacher educators' we are referring principally to the people employed by HEIs to work with 'pre-service' student teachers and on programmes of continuing professional development (CPD) on academic contracts; the type of academic worker who in the United States would in a tenure-track position and who in various countries around the world would be titled Lecturer or Senior Lecturer, Assistant or Associate Professor. Although we consider the staffing of HEI Education departments and the casualization of academic work in this chapter, we are particularly interested in how universities and colleges in England have understood the academic work of educating teachers by people with the same kind of contract and same titles as those in other disciplines such as English or engineering. We do not offer a study of the casualization of work in teacher education *per se*, although as Furlong (2013) notes, there is some evidence of increasingly casualized teacher education contracts within what is also an increasingly 'segmented labour force' (pp. 47–59).

As we said in the previous chapter, England is an interesting case internationally in terms of history, policy and the cultural identity of teachers and teacher educators. It is an example of a highly regulated, centralized, national system, subject to much more directive and frequent policy interventions than in other parts of the UK (Menter et al 2006). ITE in England has, at the graduate level, been mainly school based since 1992 (in that those students following the 1-year PGCE have spent most of their time in schools since then) and has followed a competency-based model since 1997, with national standards specified and monitored by central government and their inspectorate Ofsted. However, we believe that our analysis has relevance in many international contexts, perhaps mainly (although not entirely) English-speaking ones. In the final part of the chapter, we refer to a recent Australian study that replicated our earlier research in England with interesting results.

The data in both our own and the Australian study consisted of texts (job advertisements and job descriptions for HEI-based teacher educator positions) and talk (interviews with chairs – or heads – of HEI Education departments). Our joint focus has been on how the category *teacher educator* is produced in discourse and what that might reveal about the institutional contexts (HEIs) in which this categorization is produced. Theoretically, our perspective is grounded in sociocultural understandings of language as a mediational means and of the production and negotiation of categories as essential aspects of the cultural–historical processes that enable individuals and institutions to think and to reason together (Mäkitalo & Säljö 2003, Mercer 2000). It is consistent with and arises out of the overall CHAT orientation to our research as a whole, an approach we outlined briefly at the end of the Introduction.

Teacher educators and academic work

A distinctive population of academic workers

In the Introduction, we noted that teacher education in England was initially established in the early part of the nineteenth century, often by voluntary denominational societies. Teacher educators in these establishments were employed directly from elementary school, their practical classroom skills were prioritized over academic qualifications and they were poorly paid (Maguire & Weiner 1994). From these very early beginnings, the teacher education profession has undergone a number of changes. Notably, the passing of the Elementary Education Act of 1870 meant that there was a pressing need for the recruitment of many more teachers as many more children became entitled to a primary education. With few opportunities for financial security and independence at the time, it was educated women in particular who seized on this opportunity for employment. Maguire and Weiner (1994) note that from this time 'a distinctive occupational feminised culture developed around the job of educating teachers' (1994, p. 127). The qualifications of the population of teacher educator also improved markedly and, by 1928, 70 per cent of staff were university graduates. However, the job itself held little prestige and status, and was even held in contempt by the male-dominated culture in universities (Taylor 1969).

Before the Second World War women outnumbered men in the profession by nearly three to one in the teacher training colleges but this was to change in the second half of the twentieth century. The demands for more teachers in the 1960s led to the expansion of older colleges and the creation of new ones. During the following decades, more men were recruited as well-qualified lecturers, often at postgraduate level, and the gender balance shifted so much so that women no longer outnumbered men in the sector (Byrne 1978). Despite teacher education becoming a more 'male' profession, Taylor (1969) found that, when teacher education (for secondary school teachers) was located in universities, in comparison with other departments, Education departments were often poorly resourced and education lecturers had low status. This low status was a factor in the dilemma that faced the fictional character Prin in Andrew Davies' play; in her independent training college, Prin ruled absolutely.

In the 1980s concerns about staffing of the teacher training colleges resulted in the DES report *Teaching in Schools: the content of initial training: an HMI discussion paper* which led back to the position where 'practical experience' in teacher education came to have a higher priority (Alexander 1984, DES 1983). Teaching was conceptualized as a practical activity, simply requiring common sense and practical experience rather than the academic study of psychology, sociology and philosophy and the development of a critical or inquiring stance. Maguire and Weiner recall that this change in emphasis led to another group of people moving into the sector – teachers from state comprehensive schools whose recruitment they saw as evidence of this privileging of practical experience (1994, p. 130).

In the 2006 Economic and Social Research Council's Demographic Review of the Social Sciences in the UK (Mills et al. 2006), education was the second largest discipline under consideration and the report's authors noted the unique challenge of a large number of 'second-career researchers' – mainly, school teachers who move into universities to work on teacher education programmes. More than half the academic staff in education were found to be 50 or over at the time of the review; just under half were in the 46–55 age range, with the smallest proportion across the social sciences aged under 34 (8 per cent). The funding of higher education in the UK is partly determined by audits of the universities' research productivity and research quality across disciplines. These audits have been known as Research Assessment Exercises (RAE) and, from 2013, the Research Excellence Framework. In the 2001 exercise, the education report noted that two-thirds of education academic staff were not classified as 'research active' (Mills et al. 2006). The review suggested that the structural challenges faced by those working in education meant that 'there exists no clear academic career structure' (Mills et al. 2006, np), whereas both better career structures and higher salaries were apparent in the professional setting of schools.

Out of around ninety-six universities and colleges with Education departments in the UK, eighty-two HEIs prepared submissions to the 2008 RAE, entering 1,696 full-time equivalent staff or approximately 27 per cent of full-time staff in Education departments (HEFCE 2009a; HESA 2009). Compared with the 2001 RAE, submissions for 2008 were more selective, with 404 fewer academic staff entered (Hazlehurst et al. 2010). Indeed, 30 per cent of submissions in 2008 represented the work of fewer than ten full-time academic staff and 70 per cent represented the work of fewer than twenty (HEFCE 2009b).

Drawing on more recent HESA data, Furlong offers this summary of the demographics:

> [Education academic workers] are older than other social scientists and have shorter higher education careers because they started later; they are less likely to be recruited from ethnic minorities and non-UK nationals than other social scientists; they are more likely to be female; they are relatively low-paid; and a greater proportion of them are on teaching-only or casualized contracts. (Furlong 2013, p. 50)

The picture of education as a discipline in the UK emerging from both the demographic review and the national research audits is therefore quite dispiriting, driven in the main, we can reasonably speculate, by the presence of a large core of former school teachers for whom the possibility of developing a research programme and, indeed, progressing through a 'clear academic career structure' are fairly limited. Similar issues of research productivity and progression through the tenure track were noted in the United States by Tierney (2001) in his analysis of the National Study of Postsecondary Faculty suggesting that rather than being a purely English phenomenon, the underlying issue arises out of wider tensions between teaching (teachers) and doing research, tensions that characterize the recent history of higher education overall (cf. Cuban 1999, Jonçich Clifford & Guthrie 1988).

The distribution of teacher education work across universities in England

In the Introduction we also noted that the higher education system in England has been subject to profound change over the last 50 years. A major force for change has been the imperative to widen participation beyond the relatively small percentage of the population that had access to higher education decades ago. Many institutions that have come to have university status in England (as elsewhere around the world) grew out of specialist training colleges and, in England, that is particularly true of what has become known as the 'new university' sector. Distinct from the United States, there is currently only one private university in the UK (Buckingham); the rest are state-funded, public institutions with the same mission to produce new knowledge and to teach and engage with the wider society.

However, the 1990s also saw a move towards diversification and the establishment of a quasi-market of teacher education 'providers' in England (Mahony & Hextall 2000). Unlike in the United States, where student (consumer) demand can determine the operation of the market – with each university having a demand-led 'production function' in terms of the 'output' of teachers (Turner 2001) – in England's quasi-market, the consumer is the state that commissions specific outputs from each university. As a result, the situation in England in terms of where teacher education work is located is a complex one with programmes distributed across both old and new universities as well as in entirely school-centred (or early-entry) routes. The introduction of School Direct by the Coalition government in England in 2012 has made the situation even more complex, especially as data on recruitment (not merely recruitment targets) is hard to come by. Our anecdotal experience is that schools that have bought into the School Direct initiative in a substantial way have often partnered with regional universities for the training input (rather than elite, research-intensive universities) and that these regional universities have sometimes relied on these relatively large numbers of School Direct places as their own 'core allocation' (made directly to them by a government agency) has dwindled.

The key actor in the distribution of the places – and therefore the work – has been this agency, now known as the National College for Teaching and Leadership (NCTL), formerly the Training and Development Agency for Schools (TDA) and first established by the central government as the Teacher Training Agency (TTA) in 1992 to fund, regulate and improve recruitment into teacher education. On the basis of inspections by Ofsted and other evidence, the NCTL allocates places (i.e. per capita funding) to providers on the basis of 'target numbers'. Universities are therefore obliged to compete for funding. The allocation of places gives some sense of how teacher education work is distributed at the national level in England.

Just over half of the secondary (high school) ITE places in the 2008–2011 period (the period of this study) were allocated to the new university sector (57.3 per cent); old universities were allocated 37.5 per cent and school-centred initial teacher training schemes (SCITTS) accounted for 5.2 per cent (TDA 2009). Similarly, over 80 per cent of primary student teachers during this period underwent their professional preparation in new universities

(77.5 per cent) and SCITTS (5.9 per cent). Indeed, some new universities secured a very large proportion of the places allocated by the TDA (e.g. up to 1,392 places – or 4 per cent of the total allocation – to one large institution with multiple programmes and flexible study patterns). Since the formation of the Coalition government in England in 2010 and the introduction of the School Direct initiative, the total number of places allocated to any HEI has been cut, with significant reductions for the 2014–2015 academic year. A 15 per cent cut in direct allocations to HEIs was made at the same time as a 61 per cent increase in allocations to School Direct. While in practice, many of the students on School Direct programmes will be educated and trained by HEI-based teacher educators, the ownership of the 'place' by the schools means that the aims, design and content of the programme may well be different to that experienced by students on core, HEI-led programme (UUK 2013).

In summary, while most primary and most secondary teacher education work in England still takes place in 'new' universities (through core or School Direct allocations of places by the NCTL), these HEIs generally do less well in research funding terms and have much less concentrated research activity. In the somewhat different US context, Tierney (2001) noted that the majority of teachers were produced in the state university systems rather than private research universities, even while those private schools may offer small or 'boutique' teacher preparation programmes that are often highly regarded. To that extent, what the UK and the US have in common is that the bulk of the work of teacher education is available in public HEIs that receive funding from the state. Teacher education is still a vitally important part of the work of public universities around the world.

Researching teacher education as academic work

Academic work is most commonly defined as the labour of people employed as lecturers or professors in university settings. Indeed, Tight (2004) has identified an increasing interest in 'what lecturers and other members of staff actually do, and how this is changing' as one of the key themes in higher education research generally (p. 4). The perspective on academic work in the higher education literature is mainly sociological and has become particularly interested in how changing patterns of academic activity and employment relations are related to transnational forces of globalization and the marketization of higher education (e.g. Marginson 2010). Studies of academic work often focus on terms of employment, contractual activities and working conditions and there is a growing realization in the literature that distinctions between categories of worker in higher education are being eroded. For example, in a study of employment and working conditions for academic staff across Europe, Enders noted that 'the concept of a single academic profession might be an illusion' (Enders 2000, p. 7). It was important for our research that we kept in mind that academic work itself is not a homogeneous and undifferentiated category.

Internationally, there is little research that focuses directly on what HEI-based teacher educators actually *do* – their practical activities and the material conditions in which they labour. As Horner (2000) points out, this is not an unusual situation as academic work is often understood in an individualistic and narrowly intellectual sense (e.g. the conversation-opener, 'what are you working on at the moment?'). There has been some attention in the United States to the 'education professoriate' at the level of self-perceptions and life histories (e.g. Ducharme 1993) and their somewhat precarious status within the universities generally (e.g. Labaree 2004), and also, more generally, to the transition points between prior experience, graduate school and becoming 'faculty' (e.g. Schuster & Finkelstein 2008). Teacher educators' identities and their identity formation have also shown some growth in interest (e.g. Murray & Kosnik 2011, Olsen 2008, White 2014), mirroring interests in identity across the social sciences. This interest in the 'becoming' of university-based teacher educators and the ways in which universities as employers might support these transitions is evident in recent research literature from the UK, North America, Australia and Europe (e.g. Acker 1997, Berry 2007, Carrillo & Baguley 2011). Another line of research traces the tensions between teaching and research (e.g. Jonçich Clifford & Guthrie 1988, Tierney 2001) that are also reflected across the university (Cuban 1999, Slaughter & Rhoades 2004). Recently there has also been some specific attention to the 'gendered division of labour' in HEI Education departments whereby ITE is regarded as 'women's work' and teacher educators are positioned as the 'nurturers' and 'good citizens' (e.g. Acker and Dillabough 2007, Dillabough & Acker 2002). We discuss this line of research in the next chapter.

So while there is now a growing body of literature on teacher educators' identities, transitions in HEIs and their professional knowledge (e.g. Carillo & Baguley 2011, Griffiths et al. 2009, Murray & Male 2005, Swennen & van der Klink 2009), research into how *HEIs* – the universities and colleges – conceptualize teacher education as academic work is extremely difficult to identify. Indeed, while there is little research about what HEI-based teacher educators actually do, there is even less about what HEIs think they do. The few relevant studies are more often written from the perspective of trying to understand the teacher educator's subjectivity or professional development needs. The way in which institutions conceptualize and frame the work of teacher education is left implicit or is absent. Furthermore, other studies suggest that teacher educators themselves do not constitute a homogeneous group (Kosnick & Beck 2008, Tierney 2001). Despite this heterogeneity, the term *teacher educator* in much of the current research literature to date is treated as an undifferentiated category. A consequence of this limited conceptualization of *teacher educator* and the dearth of research generally in the field have led to rather limited understandings of the position of teacher education *as work* in higher education. The study we report on here was motivated by an interest in understanding how HEIs in England, at a particular historical moment, conceptualized teacher education as a form of academic work. Our perspective is therefore somewhat different from other researchers in this field.

In order to examine how teacher education is produced as a particular category of academic work, we decided to analyse how institutional texts and talk produce the category discursively. Our focus was on how ways of thinking about teacher education are actively produced and reproduced in institutional language. We were interested in examining the expectations and contractual requirements delivered by the job advertisement and job descriptions and in interviews with a small sample of academic leaders in HEI Education departments. Our guiding questions were:

1　How is the work of teacher education conceptualized in the job advertisements and job descriptions of a sample of vacancies?

2　How do leaders in HEI Education departments talk about the work of teacher education?

Generating texts and talk to understand categories and institutions

Design and methodology

We began by collecting job advertisements and job descriptions for all teacher education vacancies at HEIs in England during two periods totalling 8 months: July to November 2008 and March to May 2009. These periods were chosen as it was felt they represented the busiest recruitment periods for HEIs. The job advertisements and job descriptions were drawn from the website http://www.jobs.ac.uk (the main academic recruitment website in the UK) and the institutions' own websites. Job descriptions were often very complex texts including mission statements, backgrounds to the vacancy and information about the organizational structures. Our sample criteria required the vacancies to be HEI-based and to involve regular face-to-face work with students on ITE programmes.

In the period immediately following the second collection of job advertisement data in 2009, we wrote to the heads (chairs) of all the Education departments that had advertised the vacancies we had collected and requested a telephone interview. In the interview, we asked about the specific vacancy, the process of advertising and putting the further particulars texts together, how teacher education was organized and valued within the institution and other questions designed to elicit the head of department's reasoning about teacher education as academic work.

The sample of job advertisements and further particulars texts

One hundred and eleven vacancies met our sample criteria, sixty-four in the first data collection period and forty-seven in the second. The most frequent categories of vacancy were for generalist primary and secondary mathematics teacher educators (both $n = 11$ or 10 per cent). Forty-two HEIs were represented in the sample, of which thirty can be described either as 'new' universities or colleges and twelve as 'old' universities (i.e. those that had university title before 1992). Across our two samples, a greater proportion of work was available in the new university sector and, in at least one large institution, much of it on the basis of part-time and temporary employment.

Proportionately, the availability of teacher education work in the old sector was quite small and, in our samples, mostly full-time and permanent. However, it is worth striking a note of caution over the representativeness of this data as recruitment in higher education can be responsive to both demographics and policy as well as idiosyncratic.

The sample of transcribed telephone interviews

Following our letter to the heads of the Education departments that had advertised posts, eight finally agreed to be interviewed: six department chairs, one associate head of department and one director of teacher education. Although this response rate was fairly low, the intention was not to construct a representative sample. Our eight respondents came from a range of institutions: four new universities and four old, of varying sizes and in both the north and south of England. They also came from institutions that had achieved at different, although generally positive, levels in terms of research output and quality (as measured by the 2008 RAE), something we have indicated in Table 2.1 by referring to an institution's profile as greater than (+) or less than (−) the mean performance in education (which was 1.95 on a 4-point scale). Six of the HEIs represented offered ITE programmes at undergraduate (UG) as well as the graduate (G) level; the remaining two offered graduate programmes only. Although not representative, our data does begin to reflect some of the diversity of higher education settings in England.

Table 2.1 The sample of HEIs represented in the academic leader interviews

Ashland	Small, old university, south of England; UG and G RAE +
Belvoir	Medium-sized old university, south of England; PG only RAE +
Chalfont	Small, old university, north of England; G only RAE +
Dunmore	Small, old university, north of England; UG and G RAE +
Eglinton	Medium-sized new university, south of England; UG and G RAE – not entered
Finbury	Large, new university, south of England; UG and G RAE +
Gebwick	Large, new university, north of England; UG and G RAE +
Hawtree	Medium-sized new university, north of England; UG and G RAE –

Analysing texts and talk

We took a variety of analytic approaches to what constituted a relatively large amount of data in the form of texts (job advertisements and job descriptions) and talk (research interviews). One approach involved membership categorization analysis, a method of understanding how certain categories are produced in texts or the jointly constructed discourse of research interviews (Hester & Eglin 1997, Freebody 2003). Membership categorization analysis involves identifying emerging categories in the discourse, understanding how attributions are made to these categories (looking at particular verbs and adjectives, for example) and how they are substantiated (e.g. through invocation of policy discourses or through personal narratives) and then analysing how these categories and attributions permit particular conceptualizations and lines of reasoning. Lists (such as 'main duties' lists in job descriptions, for example) are a significant way in which categories are produced and, methodologically, items in such lists were seen as primary attributions to the category, in this case, the category of university-based teacher educator. In analysing the interviews, our attention was focused on how the head of department produced *teacher educator* as a category and how they used this category in their reasoning.

Although we did not set out to conduct a formal linguistic analysis, we nonetheless used a selection of analytic tools to interrogate the language data. One approach, derived from the computational strategy of corpus linguistics (McEnery & Wilson 2001), was to generate word frequencies and key-words-in-context. For example, the interviews with heads of department were analysed using computer software to generate lists of high-frequency words and collocations. The software was then used to produce key-words-in-contexts – or the stretches of discourse in which the high-frequency words appeared. This strategy gave us some insight into how the word *research* was used, for example, revealing its context in the utterances of participants.

We also drew on a linguistic annotation strategy by tagging certain word classes (e.g. nouns and verbs) in specific sentences. So, for example, we examined the corpus of advertisements and further particulars texts to identify the ways in which the job category was introduced in the first sentence of the advertisement. Initially, we focused on the word(s) that usually took the object position in this sentence – *We are looking for a* [noun or noun phrase]. The function of this clause is to orient the potential applicant towards the way in which the employer categorizes the work and the sort of knowledge, skills and experience being sought. These methods helped us to look in detail at language-in-use and complemented membership categorization analysis in order to understand how institutional conceptualizations were being built (cf. Flowerdew 2005).

Finally, with specific reference to the job advertisements and job descriptions, we conducted an analysis of them as written texts, as instances of a particular genre that share a typified rhetorical purpose (Bazerman 2004). Job descriptions and what are known in England as 'further particulars' are complex texts, emerging within institutions over often lengthy periods of time, with a recognizably similar social function. For example, while further particulars usually contain references to the specific duties of the advertised post within the Education department, they also refer to the expectations of the specific pay grade or rank across the whole university. These documents can often reveal traces of earlier versions and how conceptualizations have changed between different drafts (e.g. two sets of further particulars for two different posts in the same department). In analysing the job advertisements and further particulars as instances of genres, we looked particularly for contradictions within the texts because such contradictions can reveal the diverse ways in which the job category is understood within institutions. In other words, we did not simply assume that the advertisements and job descriptions externalized how a university was conceptualizing teacher education as academic work and our genre analysis of these texts (as well as our interviews with the heads of department) surfaced how the texts were negotiated within the institutions on the basis of different and sometimes competing priorities. For further information about our methods and analysis, see Ellis et al. (2012).

Institutional conceptualizations of the teacher educator

The shaping of categories such as that of 'teacher educator' at the institutional level to some extent precedes individual sense making, particularly when individuals are invited to align themselves with institutional motives and meanings in a job application process. To that extent, individual prospective employees are invited to 'join in' with the institutional language game. Our study did not collect and analyse workplace discourse but, consistent with a sociocultural theoretical perspective on categorization, our analysis proceeded on the basis that understanding how and where the category of teacher educator was produced in texts and talk might reveal something about the broader sociocultural traditions of conceptualization and argumentation that manifest themselves in the field of teacher education in England overall, as well as in specific institutional sites of teacher education activity.

Producing the category I: Job advertisements, job descriptions and 'further particulars'

In analysing the written texts, we quickly became aware that sectoral generalizations (i.e. between 'new' and 'old' universities) could not be warranted. A complex situation was revealed, in terms of attributions to and substantiations of the *teacher educator* category, and in contradictions in the further particulars documents. In the discussion below we have used pseudonyms to refer to sources of job advertisements as well as indicating the institutional type (new or old).

'We are looking for ... ': Introducing the teacher educator as academic worker

In many of the advertisements (46 of 111), the phrase was focused on the noun 'practitioner'. The following examples were typical of the range:

> an experienced, highly skilled *practitioner* who is passionate about their subject and has an ability to explore ideas and pose questions (Alton University – new)
>
> a *practitioner* with QTS to work on primary ITT (Downton University – old)

As 'practitioner' was rarely explained (as it is in the second example above – QTS [Qualified Teacher Status] being the professional credential in England) we inferred that what was being sought was a school-teaching practitioner. Other nouns used to orient applicants include *educator* and *pedagogue*, with *lecturer* accounting for just 3 instances out of 111. In other advertisements, beyond the academic job title in the headline, the role was not named and a different construction employed (e.g. 'In this role, you will teach on ... '). If using an acronym, advertisements referred to 'ITT' – initial teacher training – the alternative to ITE preferred by successive governments in England.

A wide range of verbs attributed activities to the job category. Teaching students is normally a significant part of the work of university-based teacher educators, as it is for academics in all disciplines. Most of the further particulars emphasized the variety of teaching required by the posts but there were many references to *training* and *delivering content*. The following examples were typical:

> *training* students on the BA course (Eldred University – old)
>
> *delivering* secondary ITT programmes (Windlesham University – new)

Initial teacher *training* has been the preferred term in policy in England since at least 1997 and *delivery* (e.g. delivering lessons) as a metaphor for teaching is common in professional discourse, especially since the introduction of the National Curriculum in 1989 (Protherough & Pick 2002).

Personal qualities were important in a significant minority of the advertisements as well as in the further particulars, leading to the elaboration of adjectives attributed to the person, before the specification of the job's main duties. Advertisements that emphasized personal qualities tended to prioritize enthusiasm, dedication and resilience. The following examples reflect these emphases:

> an enthusiastic and dedicated person (Girton University – new)
> a colleague with energy, enthusiasm and vision (Rodmell University – new)
> an excellent communicator with a positive approach for this exciting role in our challenging environment (Windlesham University – new)

The nouns used (*person*, *colleague*, *communicator*) were also interesting and there was a strong, if implicit, sense in some of the advertisements, as in the third example above, that an unusual combination of positive personal qualities would be necessary to fulfil the role successfully.

Internal contradictions in further particulars texts – and intra-institutional variations

Variation between advertisements/further particulars from the same university but different academic units (e.g. two departments in the same large school or college of education) also revealed tensions between whole-university and education conceptualizations. For example, many new universities' further particulars were characterized by elaborations of the distinction between Lecturer and Senior Lecturer grades. But *within* such institutions, there were also significant differences between whole-university and Education department discourse.

In further particulars from a new university's School of Education, for example, the main duties consisted of up to ten bullet points organized loosely around the themes of personal qualities, teaching and administrative tasks. In the same institution's School of Physical Education, the main duties were summarized in two paragraphs, focused on the kinds of teaching expected, with the administrative work linked to the activities of the institution as a whole and presented as an opportunity for 'wider involvement'. In the School of Physical Education there were also specific references to research and encouragement to potential post-holders to develop their own scholarly interests, references absent from the School of Education text. The contrast between the further particulars from these different departments within the same institution was interesting for the way in which the School of Education posts were conceived of as somewhat separate from the wider institutional context whereas the posts within the School of Physical Education seemed much more aligned with whole-university expectations delivered in the common section on expectations of Lecturers/Senior Lecturers.

The position of research in the job description's main duties list

Overall, it was rare for universities to give research priority in the first half of the main duties list, and in only one instance (at an old university) did it appear consistently throughout the initial advertisement. In this particular case, 'research and teaching' appeared throughout the details and one of the selection criteria was a 'commitment to develop high quality research output'. Two vacancies at an old university indicated that research was expected, but for one position, while research was mentioned as a priority in the job advertisement, in the main duties list 'willingness to engage in research' had fallen to 11th place. For the other post, research was at ninth place. Whilst the majority of advertisements (61 out of 111) did include research and/or scholarship as a requirement, its position in the main duties lists of the further particulars varied from 1st to 22nd. And, of course, this means that 45 per cent of the advertised posts made no reference to research at all. For readers outside the UK, the implication that research might not be regarded as a key feature of the academic work of a university-based teacher educator may be surprising but gives some sense of the distinctiveness of the English system.

As we have already indicated, intra-institutional variations were often pronounced and this was also true with respect to the position of research in the main duties list. The main duties list for the full-time, permanent vacancies in the large Faculty of Education at one new university gave research very different priorities. For example, in the main duties list for a Senior Lecturer in Primary Maths Education, the first priority was:

> 1. Lead advanced scholarship and research in the area of Primary and/or Early Years Mathematics and lead bids for research funding.

– whereas a Design and Technology position at the same level had a 'contribution' to research or 'scholarly development' as the second priority, with the field left open.

Producing the category II: The interviews with academic leaders in Education departments

Unlike the advertisements and further particulars texts, within our small sample of interviews with academic leaders, it was possible to observe differences along sectoral (new and old) lines although, as we discuss later, these differences will of course have been jointly constructed in the interview talk.

'You have to be both': The teacher educator as a hybrid category

In the interviews with heads of department or their nominees from old universities, the *teacher educator* was categorized around a tension between research productivity and quality and the potential and capacity of teacher educators to inform and influence the professional development of beginning teachers. The latter, more professional attributes were often expressed as personal dispositions towards working with teachers and with schools. This tension has been noted internationally (e.g. Berry 2007, Ducharme 1993, Jonçich Clifford & Guthrie 1988).

The Dunmore University Head of Department spoke of teacher educators as 'bridges' between 'purely academic' staff (not defined) and professional staff who only worked on ITE programmes. Teacher educators at Dunmore were positioned as a hybrid category of academic worker and one that was useful strategically in promoting the department to university senior management when Ofsted inspections resulted in excellent grades in published reports. The Ashland University Director of Teacher Education spoke about the importance of teacher educators' 'recent and relevant' school experience but also spoke of them in terms of a polarity between 'excellent teachers' and 'excellent researchers'. For the Chalfont Head of Department, teacher educators were also positioned between academics in 'very pure' disciplines (also not defined) and the 'awfully practical' world of school experience. In response to a question about what knowledge, skills and experience were privileged when making teacher education appointments, the Chalfont Head of Department gave a sense both of the hybridity of the teacher educator as academic worker and of his own positioning as a middle manager in the university:

> I am in the middle of two very hard places. One is my director of research who goes scatty if I don't demand publications, PhDs etc … on the other hand these people have to teach on PGCE [initial teacher education] programmes, so they have to be practitioners. They have to have experience in schools .… And you cannot logically expect someone who's spent half a lifetime teaching in schools … usually getting to a post of responsibility, deputy headships, that sort of thing … to have also built a good research profile and have lots of publications in (…) journals.

The Belvoir Head of Department also spoke around the challenge this presented to universities when deciding how to conceptualize the teacher educator and their work but Belvoir was distinctive in our sample because research productivity and quality were clearly privileged and a recent appointment on this basis was given as an example. The Belvoir Head of Department was also distinctive in being the only participant who made an argument – at two different points in the interview – for the importance of teacher educators' research and scholarship in student teachers' learning. Responding to a question that asked how teacher educator as a job would be explained to the general public, this Head of Department said:

> …being a really good teacher educator has to be research informed, because ideally you would want the next generation of teachers to be being taught by the leading edge in terms of knowing where the field is going. But they also need to be excellent practitioners. So I think you know you have to be both. […] Because often an excellent practitioner is heavily rooted in their own context and their own experiences. And the one real advantage of being a professional teacher educator, if you could put it like that is that, and a researcher, is that you see things from multiple perspectives … so that you can counterpoint things.

In the interviews with old university academic leaders, the teacher educator was produced as a hybrid category of academic worker requiring both research and professional credibility – an effective practitioner but one that was not situation bound. Although the Belvoir Head of Department did make an argument for the importance of research attributes in relation to professional outcomes, overall it was interesting that the importance of teacherly credibility was assumed rather than argued for.

'Quite different to other faculties': The teacher educator as an exceptional category

In the interviews with the heads of department or their nominees at new universities, teacher educator as a category was produced rather differently – as 'role models', capable of 'transferring best practice' as recognizably 'professional' figures subject to the tight constraints of policy. The Gebwick University Head of Department expressed it this way: 'our tutors have to model the best possible pedagogy, they have to be creative in their practice, set high standards of professionalism and integrity'. All four academic leaders emphasized the importance of 'successful professional experience' and all categorized the *teacher educator* by invoking official policy and managerial discourses more consistently than the old sector academic leaders. But research and scholarship as aspects of teacher educators' work were not entirely absent in these interviews. Thus, when the Eglinton Associate Head of Department was asked:

> Interviewer: [...] when you made the appointments what was it that you were privileging?
> Eglinton: We were looking for a particular academic and professional expertise in terms of a specific procurement area.
> Interviewer: Yeah.
> Eglinton: Um... we were looking for some middle management to senior experience within their existing organisation in terms of managing staff and in terms of managing curriculum development.
> Interviewer: Yeah.
> Eglinton: Um... we were looking for somebody who has got a research potential that might fit into our themed areas in terms of research within the school and within the faculty.

– the interaction illustrates both the eventual priorities that were apparent across the academic leaders in the four new universities and the development of the jointly constructed talk in the interview. These academic leaders' reasoning about research and scholarly activity was relatively more difficult to elicit in the interviews with only one of them (Hawtree) offering a rationale and strategy for research and researcher development.

Conscious that their institutional context required organized developmental activity ('we grow our own'), the Hawtree Head of Department spoke of 'research clusters' led by a professor which all new teacher educators were required to join, where they were offered research mentorship and where research targets were part of annual appraisal. The Finbury Head of Department spoke briefly of 'currently reviewing strategies for supporting research development in advance of the 2013 REF' (the forthcoming audit of research productivity) but strategic development of teacher educators' research capacity did not figure in the other two interviews. Moreover, although all these academic leaders spoke in various ways of teacher education work being 'research-informed', other than in the Hawtree interview, in response to questions about how university-level expectations of lecturers might be addressed, there was no sense of how new teacher educators (mostly straight from school teaching and without a master's degree) would *become* research-informed or sustain this capacity.

The interviews with these heads of departments also showed the extent to which they regarded the Education department as distinctive within their universities – with very different expectations of new academic staff than in other academic areas and with different institutional aims. When asked whether what was privileged in making teacher education appointments was similar to what other faculties within the university privileged, the Gebwick Head of Department responded:

> Um, no I would think we're probably quite different to most other faculties. Because we um … along with the health faculty we are looking for experienced professionals to join an educational faculty which still has a large core of its business in training initial professionals, whether it's in teaching or youth and community work or early years work. So um … we are looking for academic qualification as well as professional qualification and experience professionally. That's quite different to most other faculties.

Across these interviews, Education departments were conceptualized by the academic leaders principally as sites of teacher education 'business' and this was presented as leading to somewhat different priorities to the rest of the institution. Teacher educators were produced as an exceptional category of academic worker in this sense and also in the sense of bearing strong personal responsibilities as professional role models and exemplary practitioners.

The professional/researcher contradiction

In our sample of job advertisements and job descriptions, it was common for universities to conceptualize the teacher educator as a 'super teacher' – an effective classroom practitioner demonstrating strong personal qualities of enthusiasm and resilience. *Training* and *delivery* described teaching, often relating directly to how teaching and teacher education were described in policy and professional discourse. No significant differences were observed between new and old university sectors but differences in the way teacher educators and their work were conceptualized were often apparent *within* the same institution. For example, some posts were clearly aligned with whole-university expectations of academic work whereas obvious discontinuities were apparent between other posts and these same expectations.

Some differences were observed between how teacher educators were being categorized in interviews with the academic leaders in new and old universities but it is important to acknowledge that these differences were produced in jointly constructed talk of an interview throughout which our participants were aware of – and, in one case, explicitly referred to – our own institutional location as researchers. Nonetheless, in interviews with academic leaders in old universities, teacher educators were categorized around a contradiction between research productivity and professional credibility. The teacher educator was produced as a hybrid category of academic worker. In the interviews with academic leaders in new universities, the teacher educator was produced as an exceptional category, somewhat distinct from the rest of the institution, with different expectations made of them and different institutional goals. Although both sets of interviewees, in several respects, appeared to be managing a similar range of work (e.g. the professional preparation of teachers, CPD, research degrees) under similar resource constraints (national salary levels, national levels of student fee income) and experiencing similar kinds of personal pressure (Ofsted inspections, budgetary concerns, institutional reputation and prestige), the way in which teacher educators and their work was conceptualized in talk was different and these discursive differences related to questions of research and the capacity of teacher educators to develop a 'research profile'.

It is important for us to stress that we have been analysing publicly available texts (job advertisements and job descriptions) and research interviews with senior figures in the Education academic community in English HEIs. Although different kinds of conceptualization and argumentation are at work in the different types of data (published writing and jointly constructed interview talk), it is reasonable to assume that, taken as a whole, our data allows some insight into the ways a mixed sample of institutions conceptualize teacher education as academic work. This is not to say that our data makes institutional conceptualizations universally transparent; we do not claim that this is what these institutions think and argue always and everywhere. Given that we have to assume that decision makers in the institutions thought seriously before publishing job descriptions and that the academic leaders who answered our questions did so carefully, it nonetheless seems fair to move forward on the basis that our analysis does make it possible to comment on the ways in which the categorizations were produced and how they were used to build arguments in the public sphere about university-based teacher educators and their work.

To this extent, it is perhaps surprising that the degree to which HEIs think coherently of teacher education as academic work is fairly limited, both within and between institutions. What *is* shared is the teacher educator's difficult positioning in universities, a positioning that is produced differently in the text and talk data but reflected, for example, in a common reluctance to use the word 'lecturer' (the main academic career grade in the UK). Similarly, the institutions shared a commitment to teacher educators' credibility with the profession, usually demonstrated through significant professional experience. Indeed, this commitment to professional credibility was rather taken-for-granted.

What is not shared, it seems, is an argument for the importance of research as an aspect of teacher educators' work or for the relationship between research and teaching. Neither is an awareness of the need to develop research capacity in teacher educators, not only in relation to funding and issues of productivity but in relation to claims for research-informed teaching and student teachers' learning. In our sample of job advertisements and job descriptions and in the interviews, we found some exceptions but they were indeed exceptional rather than systemic.

We realize that one response to this interpretation of our findings is: does it matter? Perhaps wide institutional differences are what we should expect, each HEI determining their own mission and values, recruiting staff and conceptualizing teacher education as they see fit. It could be argued that there will inevitably be hierarchies of institutions like universities and colleges and hierarchies of departments, and staff within those departments, and perhaps there should be increasing acceptance of diversification according to institution type (e.g. research intensive and teaching only) and of different categories of academic worker? Twombly et al. (2006), for example, in their study of US faculty searches, ask whether the clinical faculty model – teaching staff without expectations of a research career but with a strong professional background – is worth consideration by the field as a whole. The spectre of clinical faculty in the English context was recently raised in the British Educational Research Association/Royal Society of Arts Inquiry into Research and Teacher Education (BERA 2014). And Tierney (2001), writing in the United States, explicitly argues for increasing diversity in types of HEI and types of teacher education programme.

One practical problem with adopting this model in England is that all HEIs and the work of all academic staff are regulated by the same criteria (e.g. Ofsted, research productivity and quality audits such as the REF, national quality assurance frameworks, international comparisons and rankings), with common expectations of research and teaching excellence as well as the relatively recent assumption that teachers undergoing professional preparation in one institution's programme will have an equivalent or even identical preparation to those qualifying from others. Such are the consequences of a national competency-based model of ITE within a national system of (at least, partly) public universities.

Another interpretation of our findings might be that the position of teacher educators reflects a wider situation across HEIs generally in England or at least in professional/vocational fields such as Management/ Business and Health/Social Care. Both the Economic and Social Research Council Demographic Review and our interviewees referred to potential commonalities here. It may well be the case that different conceptualizations of academic work in professional schools reflect the increasing stratification of universities in England on research lines. Certainly, on the basis of our data, it appears that what Enders referred to as the international trend across higher education of 'the rise of a class of non-professorial teachers' and 'a group of externally financed contracted research staff' is increasingly true of Education departments in England, with all the potential conflicts that this trend entails (Enders 2000, p. 23, see also Furlong 2013). That said, perhaps the situation of teacher education in England is indeed unusual: given its long history in HEIs of one kind or another (such as single-purpose training colleges), teacher education's HEI location continues to be under threat, whereas the position of relative newcomers to HEIs in England (such as Nursing and Health/Social Care) appears to be strengthening.

On the basis of the study we have reported in this chapter and the contextualizing information about the higher education sector and the changing nature of academic work, it seems reasonable to conclude that when HEIs in England think about what they are 'looking for' when recruiting teacher educators, they might want an expert 'practitioner' who can 'deliver' research-informed teaching or possibly develop a research 'profile', depending on the institutional context. This position is coherent insofar as it renders the teacher educator as a difficult or troublesome category, as hybrid or exceptional, and often the subject of some sort of truce with the university as a whole. The position lacks coherence, however, in that it doesn't attempt to reconcile what are presented as contradictory expectations nor does it argue a case for professional education in relation to higher education as a whole. While this conclusion might well be specific to the English HEIs whose institutional texts and talk we analysed, our feeling from reading the international research literature is that the problem is international.

An international perspective on the same problem: The Australian study

Over a 7-month period from September 2011 to April 2012, a group of researchers at two universities replicated our study in Australia (Nuttall et al. 2013), collecting teacher education advertisements and job descriptions from the websites http://www.seek.com.au and http://www.unijobs.com.au. As with the earlier study in England, all advertised posts had to be for HEI-based positions where working with pre-service student teachers was the principal occupation of the job. By the end of the data-gathering phase, the Australian research team was able to collect fifty-five job advertisements and accompanying institutional texts from across the sector. As before, these data were analysed so as to explore how the texts supported the cultural–

historical production and re-production of the teacher educator as a category of academic worker in the Australian context.

Analysis of the data revolved around a series of questions that sought to uncover what kind of work the texts were constructing, what kind of person was being described, what these had to say about the work of teacher education and what could be interpreted about the context that produced the texts. As in the English study, the research team also analysed language-in-use, for example, how nouns, verbs and adjectives were used to conceptualize the teacher educator.

Furthermore, in seeking to illuminate the contradictions evident within and between the job advertisement texts, in their analysis the research team was able to identify deep-seated contradictions, specifically related to the way in which the work of educating student teachers was constructed and produced. It was particularly noticeable that these contradictions seemed to be working 'effectively to erase the "teacher educator" as a category of academic work' (Nuttall et al. 2013).

What the Australian team are referring to here is the contradictory nature of the advertisements. Despite the central role of such texts being to recruit teacher educators – to attract applicants capable of educating student teachers – within the texts the term 'teacher educator' was often absent. In attempting to understand what was going on in this contradiction, the researchers suggest two processes that are at work and which radically shaped the ways in which language was used in the sample of job advertisements. The two processes Nuttall et al. (2013) describe are 'marketisation' and HR-isation' and in their analysis they argue that it is these two processes working in combination that have erased teacher education as a form of academic work.

They claim that evidence for marketization is evident within the relationship between what they refer to as the 'front-end' – in this case, the advertisement itself – and the 'back-end', that includes all of the supporting material, or what we would call the job description and further particulars. While the 'front-end' principally defines the actual role, it is the 'back-end', with all of the supporting material that provides a more detailed description of the teacher education post advertised. Whereas one might expect the 'back-end' to follow on logically from the 'front-end', in their analysis, the research team found that this was rarely the case. Rather the two types of texts were in actual fact constructing the teacher educator differently.

For example, the 'front-end' was mainly used to market the institution and hyperbole used to fulfil an advertising function. Universities would use the 'front-end' to identify and pitch themselves in order to sell their institution. But also the 'front-end' of some advertisements had a dual role: to market the institution, say as a world-leading research-intensive university, and also to appeal to potential job applicants 'by inviting them to align themselves with the institution' by contributing to its research ranking (Nuttall et al. 2013). Such institutional advertising was not restricted to research-intensive universities however. The study found that the majority of the advertisements in the sample used the 'front-end' for self-promotion in order to appeal to attractive applicants but also to market the university's image nationally and internationally, hence the researchers' use of the term marketization.

In contrast to the rampant marketization to be found in the 'front-end' of the job advertisements, in being tasked with describing the person and the work they would undertake, the 'back-end' was 'taken over by the generic descriptors associated with human resource management' (Nuttall et al. 2013) – a process the researchers referred to as HR-ization. The effect of this HR-ization has been a consequence of the domination in higher education in Australia of the 'enterprise university' (Marginson & Considine 2000).

As with our study in England, considerable hyperbole was sometimes used to describe the teacher educator, for example, phrases such as *innovative thinkers* or adjectives such as *enthusiastic*. Further similarities included the ambivalence to research found in the advertisement texts. In the 'front-end' of job advertisements, research was more prominent than it was in the 'back-end', where teaching and administration predominated. However, what emerged, and what was surprising to the Australian team, was that despite there being numerous references to the word *teaching* and the word *educator*, *teacher educator* was virtually absent from the texts.

Furthermore, there was the 'almost complete absence of specialist terms traditionally considered integral to the work of the teacher educators (e.g. pedagogy, curriculum), even in the "back-end" texts' (Nuttall et al. 2013). One needed to read between the lines or look for 'leakages' in the textual artefacts to even locate the teacher educator; indeed it was almost impossible to find any reference to what the professional knowledge base of such workers might be.

Concluding comments

Both the English and the Australian research has held that academic job recruitment texts are not simply key cultural artefacts in the HR recruitment process. They are also significant in their potential to communicate powerfully what it means to be a teacher educator in the public sphere. These textual artefacts illuminate the ways in which HEIs understand the work of teacher education. The findings from the two research studies suggest that in both English and Australian samples, the HEIs commonly conceptualized the teacher educator as a *super teacher*, a skilled classroom practitioner but a practitioner who possesses considerable personal qualities, such as enthusiasm and resilience. In England, *training* and *delivery* often described the teaching on teacher education courses and these descriptions tended to align with how teaching and teacher education are described in policy and professional discourse there. Perhaps it was no surprise then that there was a common reluctance to use the word lecturer amongst the universities in the English sample. Similarly in the Australian study, the term teacher educator and specialist terms associated with the job of teacher education were virtually absent.

In addition, what is quite stark about the study in England, and the subsequent one in Australia, was the degree to which conceptualizations of teacher education as academic work lacked any meaningful coherence. In both samples there were marked differences in the way in which teacher educators and their work were described. There was, for example, little agreement about the importance of research as an aspect of teacher educators' work and considerable equivocation about the relationship between research and teaching. The analysis of all of the data did highlight the fact that research mostly appeared to be either a minimal or a vague expectation and in some instances was virtually absent in descriptions of teacher educators' work. This ambivalence to research found in institutional texts, we would argue, acts powerfully to conceptualize teacher education as a form of semi-academic work. Such framing of the work of teacher education does little to rectify what some have argued is its 'vanishingly low status and influence within the academy' (McNicholl & Blake 2013). But perhaps the most worrying feature was to be found in the Australian sample of job advertisements. In this sample, the conceptualization of the work of teacher education did not merely lack logic and coherence, the teacher educator as an academic worker had disappeared. As the research team concluded, by avoiding an 'energetic portrayal of the job being advertised', 'the actualities of the work' had been airbrushed out (Nuttall et al. 2013).

This position surely renders teacher education as a troublesome category, be it a hybrid or exceptional category. Arguably, failure to reconcile what we have found in our data to be contradictory expectations of teacher educators and their work makes the current position of universities incoherent. Furthermore, this position does little to prepare for any reconfiguration of the future practices of teacher education in higher education – a reconfiguration that appears to be increasingly required and overdue, in England and perhaps elsewhere.

3

Teacher Educators at Work: The Division of Labour

This chapter begins by briefly examining the available research literature on the work of school-based teacher educators – known in different countries as 'mentors' or 'supervising' or 'cooperating' teachers – before reporting on a year-long, mixed methods study of the work of HEI-based teacher educators – their activities, social organization and material conditions, as well as the teacher educators' own accounts of their work (for the final report, see Ellis et al. (2011)). The chapter therefore focuses on the concept of *division of labour* in ITE – the work that takes place in schools and that which takes place in universities, as well as the division of labour within HEI Education departments where certain forms of work are available to some academic workers (e.g. research and research degree supervision) and other forms of work to others (ITE). The chapter raises questions about how this division of labour has come about. As we stated in the Introduction, our interest in this book is to examine what goes on in higher education in the name of teacher education as a step on the way to suggesting ways in which this activity might be reconfigured. So our attention to the work of school-based mentoring and supervision is, in this context, brief.

The literature on the work of school-based teacher education has, perhaps, been most successful in coming up with models of mentoring and supervision rather than unpicking the social and material complexities of mentoring as more experienced teachers' work with teacher-students. Research on mentoring has also highlighted the tensions between social support and assessment of competence by mentors of trainees in the workplace and on the difficulties of establishing social spaces within schools for open and critical dialogue about matters of pedagogy. This difficult situation for interaction in schools between HEI-based teacher educators, school-based mentors and student teachers has become exacerbated by the degree to which school and HEI cultures have become infected by the GERM of neoliberalism (Ball 2012).

The research we report on HEI-based teacher educators – conducted with Allan Blake and Jim McNally – shows how, under conditions of academic capitalism (Slaughter & Rhoades 2004), the academic workers in our sample were denied opportunities to accumulate capital (e.g. research publications, grants) and were instead subject to a form of proletarianization, turning them into a highly flexible population of workers, responsive to market pressures and deprived of the capacity to appropriate surplus value from their labour. The reasons for this stratification among academic workers were complex and structural but, in our analysis, we suggest that the importance of maintaining relationships with schools, and between schools and student teachers, in the name of 'partnership' teacher education was highly significant but also that the historical cultures of teacher education as an activity of higher education must be considered. Consequently, the chapter also pays attention to the research, such as it is, on school-based and HEI-based teacher educators working together on the learning and development of new teachers.

Teacher educators: Changing roles and different contexts

As we saw in the previous chapters, the reforms during the 1980s and 1990s in England led to all ITE programmes establishing partnerships between universities and colleges and schools. Concomitantly, these reforms stipulated that students spend the majority of their time in school and at the same time some of the funding was diverted away from higher education and into schools. In this partnership model, inevitably the role of school-based teacher educators in the education and training of student teachers grew and the role of the university-based teacher educator (sometimes known as a 'tutor') changed and, in some senses, diminished. In itself, the increased role for school-based teacher educators did not directly lead to the HEI tutors' role diminishing. Rather, one might say it was the financial squeeze caused by the associated funding cuts that were particularly instrumental in this process. As higher education came to view the face-to-face work with school colleagues to be in John Furlong's words 'an expensive luxury' (1996, p. 50), money was saved by reducing tutor visits to schools so that their role became aligned with the monitoring of the training provision and assuring its quality.

Although ITE partnerships have existed for many years now, each with their own partnership agreements identifying roles and responsibilities shared between universities/colleges and schools, there still remains a lack of clarity about the division of labour, particularly which elements of partnership in ITE impact on student teachers (Moyles & Stuart 2003). In some senses, the division of labour in ITE partnerships continues to be determined by the rather unbalanced partnerships that arose out of the reforms (Furlong et al. 2000). Simply put, while HEIs have been obliged to involve schools in their ITE programmes, there is no such obligation on schools to get involved – they can more or less choose to opt in or out as they please.

This imbalance in partnerships sees HEIs taking responsibility for the quality of its outcomes and HEI-based teacher educators becoming the means by which this is achieved and schools, inevitably focused upon pupils and their achievements, less accountable but having the major role (in terms of time and closeness to practice) in student teacher development. Despite this imbalance, schools, as well as HEIs, do have recognizable key players who have specified roles and responsibilities. In ITE partnerships in England, the two key people are the HEI-based teacher educator or tutor (the Lecturer in Education) and the school-based cooperating teacher, or mentor (often but not always an experienced teacher). Mentors, unsurprisingly given the amount of contact time they have with student teachers, have been identified as not merely *a* key player but *the* key player in the professional development of students (Hobson 2002). However, Hobson also points out that the quality of the mentoring students in England receive is variable, possibly because for schools the training of student teachers is not their primary priority. In some schools the needs of student teachers might be given a worryingly low priority (Evans et al. 1996, Maynard 1996) or in others, such needs are poorly understood.

Where this is the case, school leaders might then select mentors not because they possess the necessary qualities and skills but simply because they have space on their timetables (Bullough & Draper 2004) or because they are excellent teachers, ignorant of the fact that as mentors they might struggle to articulate and open out their practice for others to see (Hobson 2002, Maynard 1996). Alternatively, limited mentoring skills could be due to inadequate preparation and training (Early 1993) or in the minds of mentors, school priorities and values override the education of their mentees (Ingleby & Tummons 2012).

The central role that mentors have in the education and training of student teachers has been replicated in much of the literature with a focus upon the impact of the mentor on student teacher development (e.g. Britzman 2003, Rich & Hannafin 2008). Much less has been written and published in relation to the role of the HEI-based tutor, including the ways in which they work with mentors and students in school. In the following section we consider the recent research that has explored the activities of school-based teacher educators (mentors or supervisory teachers) as well as the much smaller body of work that looks at the interactions of HEI- and school-based workers as they work together in initial education programmes.

The work of school-based teacher educators

The wealth of studies pertaining to the role, responsibilities and purpose of mentoring in ITE around the world, has not, however, fully unpicked the complexities of what occurs in school. For mentors, it sometimes seems that their principal aim is to take 'the "raw" goods that university sends them' and to help 'fledgling teachers develop and evolve into a finished product' (Abell et al. 1995, p. 178). Models of mentoring have also been defined. Maynard and Furlong (1993), for example, identified three different models: the 'apprenticeship model' where the mentor is the master teacher to be emulated; the 'competence model' where the mentor directs training in relation to standards of practice and the 'reflective model' where the mentor adopts a role as 'critical friend'. In other words, the role of the school-based mentor can range from merely 'being there' in order to be emulated (Feiman-Nemser et al. 1993) or to actively assisting student teachers, by for example scaffolding learning by 'listening, modelling teaching and analysing and discussing practice and providing constructive criticism' (Edwards & Collison 1996, pp. 27–28). In many national contexts, commonly the role of the mentor is seen to be that of a 'support', an 'expert' and a 'critical friend' (Furlong et al. 2000, Maynard & Furlong 1993).

However, tensions exist for mentors as they strive to be both supportive and critically constructive. It is why collaborative mentoring, involving co-planning and teaching, where mentor and mentee relationships are built on mutual trust and openness, is espoused.

Notwithstanding this, Ingelby and Tummans (2012) warn, the climate in England – with an emphasis upon individual teachers and their 'output data' – will surely only negate attempts for collaborative work in ITE in schools.

The challenges that mentors face in trying to be both supportive and critical are also complicated by particular cultural norms that exist. In a cross-national comparison, it was found that, in contrast to German mentors, English mentors valued supportiveness above honesty in their interactions with student teachers (Jones 2001), in part, to avoid hurting feelings (Maynard 2000) but also because, the researchers speculate, in England 'getting on with people' is deemed to be more important than frankness (Tomlinson 1998, p. 58). Further tensions can arise if mentors are also expected to take responsibility for the summative judgments of student teachers' competence; too cosy relationships with mentees can 'muddy the waters' and challenge mentors' objectivity (Fransson 2010, Smith 2000). Moreover, when assessment forms part of the mentors' role, stress is put on the product of mentoring rather than the actual process; rather than mentoring being developmental, it becomes 'judgmental or linked to standards and targets' and this leads to an erosion of more collaborative ways of working (Ingelby & Tummans 2012, p. 173).

Despite these concerns, however, Hobson (2002) reminds us that the evidence of the detrimental effect of linking assessment and mentoring 'remains inconclusive' (p. 213). Indeed studies have indicated that while challenging, mentors are able to support and assess student teachers simultaneously, providing the relationship as a critical friend is well established (Yusko & Feiman-Nemser 2008). For student teachers, while it is crucial that their mentors are supportive, reassuring and 'prepared and able to make time for them, to offer practical, advice and ideas relating to their teaching' (Hobson 2002, 16), they also value constructive criticism (Moran et al. 1999) and do not seem to have an issue with their mentors having a dual role (Rippon & Martin 2006). In the United States, evidence has emerged that the dual role is in fact beneficial in giving mentors a 'clearer sense of the direction of their mentoring' (Carver & Feiman-Nemser 2009, 317); for example, the use of standardized assessment tools can help guide mentors' practice.

School- and HEI-based teacher educators working together

In England, the responsibility for the assessment of student teachers is often shared between HEI-based tutors and school-based mentors. However, across the different institutional boundaries, there are some differences in this division of labour. In some partnerships, HEIs are reluctant to let go of their role in the assessment of students; in others, this responsibility falls upon schools and the university or college has little more than a moderating role (Williams & Soares 2000). Both present challenges, not least because, for mentors with their relationships with students, they might struggle to be sufficiently objective and, for HEI-based teacher educators, with their limited contact with students, they have a limited evidence base to make accurate judgments (Christie et al. 2004). Therefore, in many ITE partnerships the assessment of student teachers is the joint responsibility of the HEI and the school – for example, when tutors, mentors and students come together in school in order to monitor progress and assess competence. The ways in which these three parties interact and work together are relatively under-researched. However, in the following section we discuss some of the recent literature that has looked at this question.

Unlike the plethora of studies focused upon mentors and their impact on student teachers, little work has looked at the HEI-based lecturer and their work in schools interacting with students and mentors. While sometimes being positioned as a 'boundary spanner' whose aim is to bridge the gap between theory learnt in the university and the practical knowledge acquired during school placements, HEI-based teacher educators practice remains 'elusive and shadowy' (Cuenca 2010, p. 263) – one of the reasons why we have been so keen to document what it is that HEI-based teacher educators actually do. The existing research that has explored these questions further presents a rather mixed picture, particularly, in relation to the HEI-based tutor's contribution to student teachers' development. While earlier studies argued that the tutors' role was crucial in helping students to look critically at their own practice (Furlong et al. 2000), two later studies in England showed that the majority of students perceived their mentors rather than their HEI-based tutors to be the most significant 'other' during their ITE programmes (Hobson 2002, Hutchinson 2008). This is hardly a surprising finding given that mentors commonly have daily contact with their mentees, whereas tutors invariably have much more limited interactions with them while on school placements (Fletcher & Barrett 2004, Guyton & McIntyre 1990).

Further, the reduction in face-to-face working in school is exacerbated by partnership working and by the heavily, bureaucratic, competency-based regime that exists in England. Often, it has been observed, tutors have little more than a 'troubleshooting, interventionist function' (Blake et al. 1997, p. 138) where the 'need for diplomacy, for skills in cementing relationships between mentors and students in school' is paramount (Blake et al. 1997, p. 198).

Despite this situation, when HEI-based tutors visit schools they do not merely represent a 'friendly face' (MacDougall et al. 2013). There are still opportunities for some significant interactions with students and students do value HEI-based tutors' visits to school in providing an 'alternative' perspective and in supporting their development as beginning teachers (Williams & Soares 2000). However, other than studies that have explored students' perspectives, little work has been able to substantiate the claim that HEI-based tutor visits to school have a positive impact on student teacher learning. In fact, it has been suggested that HEI-based teacher educators' lack of impact is due to the interactions between tutors and students being complicated by a third party – the mentor – within what is termed the 'triad' (Hopper 2001, Martin et al. 2011).

Viewed positively, triads – the three-way observation and discussion between student, mentor and HEI-based teacher educator, a common feature of ITE – provide a forum for a trade of practice (Hopper 2001). And while clearly important in ITE, little research has looked at the working of triads – or into how school-based mentors, student teachers and HEI-based tutors interact and work within them (Martin et al. 2011). The studies that do exist show us that triads can be unique (Douglas 2009) and their dynamics can be fluid and complicated – or even conflicted – as the different people – each with their own priorities, values and intentions – negotiate and position themselves (Cartaut & Bertone 2009). To some extent, triads have been shown to be rather ineffective in enhancing student teacher learning because of their inevitably hierarchical nature (Koerner, Rust and & Baumgartner 2002, Zeichner 2010). For example, differentials in power between school-based mentors and HEI-based tutors can help undermine efforts in establishing open and honest collaborative dialogue. Students, in particular, being positioned at the bottom of the hierarchical structure, can feel unable to engage in open and critical discourse. If this situation continues and positions of power are not successfully negotiated, particularly between the HEI tutor and school mentor, then student teachers can end up being stuck in the middle of a conflict, which can lead to the triad failing with dire consequences for the student teachers' development (Bullough & Draper 2004). Unresolved power conflicts can be complicated by a lack of shared understandings about classroom pedagogies and student teacher learning. One study showed that students, mentors and tutors, each with differing intentions and priorities, viewed the same episode of teaching very differently (Tillema 2009). Another study found HEI-based tutors and school-based mentors holding conflicting views about how to help student teachers plan lessons (Valencia et al. 2009).

Triads can also be difficult social spaces because often 'the roles and role expectations held by the three parties often are unclear and also shifting', only exacerbated by the poor communication seen in some triads (Bullough & Draper 2004, p. 407, also see Slick 1997). Communication in a triad can fail for different reasons: students might keep their frustrations with their school placements to themselves (Maynard 2000; Valencia et al. 2009); tutors, unwilling to change the schools in which they place students, rather than voice concerns, manage and alleviate problems as they arise (Ducharme 1993, Valencia et al. 2009). Moreover, mentors, to protect their relationships with mentees, might struggle to be sufficiently open, honest and frank (Jones 2001). It seems that, in triads, what happens is that everyone expends energy and effort managing those all-important relationships while simultaneously stifling real debate and discussion about practice. For these reasons, is it any wonder that some question the capacity of traditional triads as a forum for critical explorations of pedagogy?

While perspectives are likely to differ in any triad, consensus might not be necessary. Triads can work most effectively when members recognize and honour different viewpoints (Nguyen 2009). Some studies have shown, however, that rather than resolving conflicts, honouring different viewpoints, settling conflicts of power, there is some sort of collusion going on in some triads. Student teachers, it seems, can be adept at 'negotiating the terrain' so that HEI tutors remain ignorant of any conflicts they have with mentors and with less than ideal school practices. At the same time, HEI-based tutors keep concerns hidden for fear of upsetting school colleagues and damaging the student–mentor relationship; mentors' closeness to their mentees, mean that their honesty is compromised (Martin et al. 2011). Although the avoidance of conflict is understandable, particularly for university tutors whose remit is largely to maintain relationships with school partners, when triadic parties collude in this way there are serious consequences. As Valencia et al. (2009) in their study found, all that collusion results in is each member of the triad being 'pulled off-course, losing an opportunity to benefit personally from student teaching experience and leaving the student teacher at risk' (p. 320).

In England, positive relationships between HEI-based tutors, mentors and schools are 'at the very heart of school-based training' (Hopper 2001, p. 220) and the obligation to involve schools means that maintaining relationships with school colleagues and hence securing the partnership are paramount for HEI-based teacher educators. This way of working, however, means that tutors are constantly constrained by the 'need to tread a diplomatic and sometimes delicate path' (Hopper 2001, p. 219) to maintain those all-important relationships and in so doing, 'help minimise the limitations and maximise the undoubted benefits of professional placements' (Hopper 2001, p. 221). From our own experience as teacher educators, we know that tact and diplomacy can be central to maintaining good working relationships in ITE partnerships in England. However, as was the case for the students in Valencia et al.'s study, our feeling was that an over-abundance of tact and diplomacy can limit criticality and lead to collusion in triads that can deny students 'opportunities to develop deeper understandings of conceptual and pedagogical tools' and 'to engage professionally with their mentors about problems of practice' (Valencia et al. 2009, p. 313, also see Douglas 2009).

Understanding the limitations of the current interactional possibilities within triadic teacher education work in schools, led us once again to consider the work of the HEI-based teacher educator and the ways in which their labour is framed by the value systems of higher education overall.

Academic work, academic capitalism and HEI-based teacher education

As we discussed in the previous chapter, while there has been some recent, specific attention to teacher education as academic work, the research literature is still developing. In Canada, Acker and Dillabough (2007) and Dillabough and Acker (2002) studied teacher education as 'women's work', subject to a 'gendered division of labour' that positions them as the 'good citizens' and 'nurturers' of university Education departments (2007, p. 300–301). Earlier, Maguire (1993, 2000), in England, had shown how 'the job of educating teachers' fell disproportionately onto women who have been more subject to regulation by new regimes of HEI funding as well as to historical forms of social control. Liston's (1995) analysis of teacher education work in US schools of education concluded that it constituted the 'domestic labour' of such institutions and, as such, was an effect of systemic segregation that had 'created a "classed" system of labour in schools of education that harms, not hinders, the education of teachers' (p. 91).

Generally, as we have already said, research into teacher educators as academic workers has focused on questions of identity (e.g. Murray & Male 2005, Swennen & van der Klink 2009), professional lives and career transitions (e.g. Carillo & Baguley 2011, Ducharme 1993) and induction needs, most especially concerned with research development (e.g. Griffiths et al. 2009, Murray 2005). Studies that have treated teacher education as work have often made gender a central focus of their analysis or have regarded labour mainly as an institutional concept, through which individual workers add value to institutional assets. Elsewhere in the higher education research literature, however, lines of inquiry over the last 15 years have increasingly situated academic work within a set of social relations described as academic capitalism.

Academic capitalism and higher education

Slaughter and Leslie (1997) defined academic capitalism, in the US context, as 'the pursuit of market and market-like activities' (p. 17), a process they saw reflected in inter-institutional competition over tuition fees, competition over grant income and the commercial significance of intellectual property rights. Rhoades and Slaughter (1997) also suggested that individual academic workers are invited to become '"capitalist entrepreneurs" in order to survive or thrive within the system' (p. 33). Based on their success in accumulating academic capital (grants, patents, prizes, endowments, etc.), Rhoades and Slaughter argued, they are 'differentially invested in' by the institution in a way that mirrors the privatization and deregulation of the higher education system as a whole. In Slaughter and Rhoades' (2004) book, academic capitalism had led to a 'blurring of boundaries among markets, states and higher education'; their earlier analysis of intellectual property was extended to all the 'core academic functions', including teaching and research, with consequential changes in contracts and employment relations (Slaugher &

Rhoades 2004, p. 11). Developments in higher education in England have led to similar analyses (e.g. Holmwood 2011), including comparisons with the United States (Tuchman 2009).

Capital accumulation and proletarianization

Eagleton (2011) reminds us that 'it is to Marxism that we owe the concept of different historical forms of capital' (p. 2). Capital, for Marx, was not a thing; capital was *value* and it was the means of production of value that was key. Capitalism was the social relations within which commodities achieve value and Marx saw this as an antagonistic struggle: 'as capital is accumulated by the bourgeoisie, labourers are proletarianised' (Marx & Engels 1888/2008, p. 9). Within this process, commodities are seen to have two different kinds of value: use value and exchange value. Marx's particular interest was in exchange values as these helped him reveal the capitalist relations of production and consumption (Harvey 2010). Moreover, exchange value in commodities is 'congealed' human labour (Marx 1887/1992, p. 142). In other words, it is not merely a specific type of labour that can congeal value in a commodity but a specific type of *social relations*–exchange relations, in which the value achieved by labour and materialized in the commodity can be capitalized.

Although arising from an analysis of urban, manufacturing society in the mid-nineteenth century, and the far-reaching consequences of the industrial revolution, Marx's two-sided process of capital accumulation and proletarianization, and antagonistic relations between the bourgeoisie and wage labourers, was never confined to top-hat wearing entrepreneurs and industrialists, factory workers and peasants. In *The Communist Manifesto*, Marx and Engels had already noted that the bourgeoisie 'has converted the physician, the lawyer, the priest, the poet, the man of science, into its wage labourers' (Marx & Engels 1888/2008, p. 6). Debord noted 'the extension of the logic of the factory labour to a large extension of "services" and intellectual professions' (Debord 1977, p. 114). Harvey has recently pointed to 'an insidious process of proletarianisation' of the medical workforce and in higher education (Harvey 2010, p. 279). In other words, academics as a category of HEI-based worker are at risk of proletarianization even while some might survive or thrive.

Guillory, in a groundbreaking study of academic work in the humanities, refers to academic staff situated within a 'theoretical torsion' between alternatives of capitalization and proletarianization:

> ... the torque embodied in intellectual labour can be released in [either] direction.... This is to say that knowledge, like money, is only capital

when it is capitalised, when it produces the effect of *embourgeoisement*; and conversely, that knowledge can be devalued in such a way that its possessors become indistinguishable from wage-labour – a process of proletarianisation. (Guillory 1994, p. 125)

This torsion revolves around the kinds of work that are valued and those that are devalued. Under conditions of contemporary academic capitalism, work that produces research publications, grant income, endowments and so on can be capitalized in the marketplace for promotion, salary increases, release from teaching and other effects of academic *embourgeoisement*. Work that doesn't achieve surplus value leaves the worker vulnerable to downward social mobility, the 'vicissitudes of competition, to all the fluctuations of the market' (Marx & Engels 1888/2008, p. 9). We will argue that the teacher educators in our sample have become particularly vulnerable to this process. Indeed, we wish to suggest that the concept of proletarianization is worth examining again with reference to the labour of teacher educators just as it was examined in relation to teachers in the 1980s (e.g. Ball 1988, Lawn & Ozga 1988).

Teacher education, higher education and performance-based funding of research in the UK

Teacher education in England has evolved around partnerships with schools, most often in the geographic area immediately surrounding HEIs. Since 1992 (DES 1992), these partnerships between HEIs and schools have been the statutory organizing principle around which programmes have been designed. In neighbouring Scotland, without this statutory organizing principle, cooperative partnerships between schools and HEIs have also developed (cf. Christie 2003) and in both countries student teachers and teacher educators are required to cross the boundaries of different higher education and school activity settings. In his research through the 1990s and into the 2000s, Furlong noted both the potential and the challenge of building genuine 'collaborative' partnerships between schools and universities where the pedagogical and epistemological assumptions of both partners might be questioned (Furlong et al. 2000). Instead, he found that more bureaucratic, HEI-led partnerships have evolved where universities became responsible for monitoring and quality assuring the enculturation of student teachers into the existing practices of the host school (Furlong et al. 2009b).

As we have stressed, historically, teacher education in England has developed alongside profound systemic changes to higher education overall, with independent colleges gradually being absorbed into polytechnics or universities. A similar process took place in Scotland where the large monotechnic colleges of education were also merged into the universities through the 1990s (Kirk 1999). As a result, in both countries within the UK, there are academic workers in university Education departments who began their careers in very different sorts of institutions, often without a history of research activity (cf. Maguire 1993, Murray et al. 2009). Across the UK, universal auditing of research productivity and quality began with the Research Assessment Exercise (RAE) of 1992 and subsequent exercises have further intensified the competition between institutions and individuals for publication outlets, research funds and indicators of esteem. The RAE and its successor the Research Excellence Framework (REF) have measured both the productivity and the quality of research by academics across all subject areas and disciplines. Minimum levels of research productivity have been set and minimum levels of quality for each output too (currently, usually between two and three stars, with four stars the highest 'world-leading' acclamation). Aggregated productivity and quality data produced through a lengthy peer review process, combined with other information such as research grant income, determine a numerical grade (or GPA, grade-point average) for each department in each university. On the basis of the GPA, that department is differentially funded for research over the next several years.

Fourteen years ago, Elton (2000) had already identified several unintended consequences of the RAE, such as a 'transfer market' for those who have thrived in the system, a proliferation of journals for research 'outputs', pressure on individual academic workers to be and remain consistently research active over a career, and the devaluation of teaching. Indeed, Tuchman (2009) has argued against replicating the UK RAE in the United States, citing its impact on the kind of knowledge that is created through academic work. Nonetheless, the measurement of academic workers' research productivity and quality has become entrenched in higher education systems in several other parts of the world, including the Excellence in Research in Australia initiative (http://www.arc.gov.au/era/) and New Zealand's Performance-based Research Fund (http://www.tec. govt.nz/Funding/Fund-finder/Performance-Based-Research-Fund-PBRF-/). In both these countries, there are also similar histories of single-purpose teacher training colleges becoming part of multi-campus research-intensive universities in the last 30 to 40 years (e.g. The University of Newcastle [NSW] 2008), and in some cases more recent mergers such as those in New Zealand that saw a college such as Auckland College of Education become incorporated into the research-extensive University of Auckland

(2004). As others have argued (e.g. Murray & Male 2005, Murray et al. 2009), it is teacher educators who have been particularly vulnerable to the negative consequences of exercises such as the RAE to which they have become subject as their institutional contexts – as well as the overall value systems of higher education – have changed (and not just those at the start of their careers).

The 'Work of Teacher Education' study

The research we are reporting on in this chapter was part of a study funded by the UK Higher Education Academy called the 'Work of Teacher Education' (WoTE). The WoTE project responded to a themed call for proposals about 'Teacher education for the twenty-first century', and one of the criteria for evaluation was that the research included at least two countries of the UK. We chose to work with colleagues at the University of Strathclyde in Glasgow – Jim McNally and Allan Blake – and to look at the same research questions in the English and Scottish educational contexts. Although spanning the border between the two countries, we did not set out to conduct a truly comparative study.

In terms of design, we adopted a mixed methods approach that included semi-structured interviewing, statistical analysis of data from a work diary instrument, ethnographic-type observation and a participatory data analysis workshop. Our research was guided by the following research questions:

1 What is the HEI-based teacher educator's work? What are their typical, professional activities and what are the material (social and cultural) conditions in which they are situated? (What do they do?)

2 How do the HEI-based teacher educators talk about their work? (*How do they talk about what they do?*)

In designing our research, we intended to focus our analytic attention on social organization of the WoTE and, in particular, the key CHAT categories of *rules*, *community* and *division of labour* – fundamentally, who gets to do what work and why? As with any CHAT analysis, however, these categories are not viewed in isolation but in relation to the people doing the work (the *subjects*, their desires, dispositions and motives) and the potentially shared *object* (goal and outcome) of their joint activity, an object that might be transformed (Engeström 2007a).

Data generation and analysis

Constructing the sample

We distributed a call for participation through a variety of channels in March 2010, specifying our sample criteria: we were looking for HEI-based teacher educators in England and Scotland who had direct responsibility for working with student teachers and schools on pre-service teacher education programmes. We received twenty expressions of interest by our deadline. Four of these did not meet our selection criteria. We invited sixteen respondents to an initial meeting in May 2010 and fourteen attended. Soon after, another participant withdrew following promotion. Information about the final sample is shown in Table 3.1.

The institution column shows whether, in England, the participant was employed by a 'new' university (given the title after 1992), an 'old' university or in one of the large further education colleges (FE – similar to a US community college) with higher education provision. The highest qualification column indicates whether the participant held a doctoral (D), a master's (M) or a bachelor's degree (B). 'M s' in this column indicates someone who was enrolled as a doctoral student. A tick in the research active column indicates a participant who was working towards submission in the REF and/or had been entered in the 2008 RAE.

Sampling was purposive as we sought to recruit participants from a range of institution types, geographic areas and with different career lengths. Our sample was not intended to be representative of the population of HEI-based teacher educators in England and Scotland. According to figures from the Higher Education Statistics Agency (HESA) available at the time of sampling (HESA 2009), 63.1 per cent of academic workers in UK Education departments are female. In our sample, eleven out of thirteen participants (84.6 per cent) were women. That said, HESA does not differentiate between fields within subject areas so it is possible that the distribution of women in teacher education (rather than Education as a whole) is higher than 63.1 per cent. HESA data, the Economic and Social Research Council (ESRC) Demographic Review (Mills et al. 2006) and the RAE 2008 report (HEFCE 2009a, 2009b) nevertheless suggest that the levels of academic qualification and research activity of our participants are broadly typical. Our sample also reflected a range of experience (with roughly equal proportions of participants with more than 10 years experience, more than 4 years experience and less than 4 years experience). A range of subject emphases was also present and, although the sample appeared to be biased mainly towards secondary teacher educators, in fact five of the nine nominally secondary participants also taught on primary (elementary education) courses.

Table 3.1 The sample of teacher educators

No.	Pseudonym	Gender	Institution	Main phase/ subject area	Years in HE	Highest qualification	Research active
1	Sally	F	England – OLD	Secondary – English	2	M s	√
2	Brendan	M	England – NEW	Primary – History	6	M	
3	Anne	F	England – OLD	Secondary – Science	<1	M	
4	Daisy	F	England – FE	Secondary – Science	18	M	
5	Martha	F	England – NEW	Secondary – Geography	19	D	
6	Jo	F	England – OLD	Secondary – Science	4	M s	√
7	Joyce	F	England – FE	Primary – History	17	B	
8	Natalie	F	England – NEW	Primary – Maths	1	D	
9	Duncan	F	Scotland	Secondary – Maths	7	B	
10	Miranda	F	Scotland	Primary – General	4	M	
11	Moira	F	Scotland	Secondary – Geography	3	M s	√
12	Michelle	F	Scotland	Secondary – Geography	5	M s	√
13	Iain	M	Scotland	Secondary – Music	17	B	√

Interviews

All participants were interviewed in May 2010 with our questions designed to elicit their talk about their work, their educational biography and employment history and their sense of their future. Audio recordings of the interviews were transcribed. Two analytic passes were made. The first, by three members of the research team, made a life history analysis using concepts from life history research derived from Mandlebaum (1973; see also Goodson 2008). This analysis revealed how the participants talked about their trajectories of social practice – the turning points and adaptations made and how these related to their work conditions. The second pass involved membership categorization analysis (MCA) (Freebody 2003, Hester & Eglin 1997), an approach to analysing language data we took in the research reported in Chapter 2. MCA analyses the attributions made to particular categories in the discourse of research interviews (e.g. the verbs and adjectives), the ways these attributions are substantiated (e.g. through personal narrative or invocation of policy texts) and what lines of reasoning these attributions and substantiations afford.

Work diaries

Participants were asked to complete a work diary instrument. This involved keeping a record of activity in increments of 1 hour for the duration of what was, for participants, a 'typical' working week (up to 7 days). Data was collected at two points in the year: May and October 2010. We selected these time points as it was felt they reflected the different types of work undertaken by teacher educators in the UK over an academic year: in May, most student teachers would be out on full-time field placements in schools (and be visited by teacher educators); and in October, most student teachers would be mainly based in the HEI, taking classes. All participants completed the May 2010 instrument. One participant, Iain, did not complete the second.

The diaries were divided alphabetically according to participants' pseudonyms into two sets. Working individually, we made a list of the activities of the teacher educators as they had recorded them. This process resulted in a total of seventy items, which contained numerous duplications. The two lists were reviewed, and the items grouped into a reduced number of thirty-two categories, from which a final combined list of ten job dimensions was agreed. The second set of work diaries was also analysed using this framework; no supplementary definitional precision was called for during this round of analysis, nor were further job dimensions required to be created.

In this way, for each of the weeks recorded, the number of hours allocated by the teacher educators to each of the job dimensions could be calculated. The statistical outcomes from this process were then examined in relation to fieldwork data from observation/work-shadowing. Questions about these initial job dimensions were generated by the research team and taken to the participatory data analysis workshop. As an outcome of this analysis workshop with participants, some of the job dimensions were renamed to reflect more accurately the nature and purpose of the work being categorized. The final list of job dimensions was:

1 Course management

2 Personnel activities

3 External examination at another institution

4 Examination at own institution

5 Marking

6 Professional development

7 Research

8 Relationship maintenance

9 Working with a group of students (teaching)

10 Tutoring an individual student (academic supervision, lesson observation/de-briefing)

A comparison of the data suggested that despite being 6 months apart in time, the 2 weeks may be broadly comparable in terms of work categories recorded and effort expended.

Participant observation – 'work shadowing'

We planned to observe all thirteen participants for at least one working day. They were asked to choose a 'typical' day – typical in terms of the range of work planned at that time of year, October 2010 to January 2011. We made field notes – including some near-verbatim reconstructions of spoken interaction – and also took photographs. Due to severe weather conditions in Scotland in winter 2010/2011, Miranda was not observed.

Field notes and photographs from each observation were written into narrative form. These narratives were then collated and the entire set subject to an initial, inductive coding. Two further codings of the data set were made. The first used categories derived from CHAT. Particular attention was given to the socio-historic organization of the activities in which the teacher educators were engaged – how the work was organized and between whom (the division of labour and the social conventions). The second coding used the ten job dimension categories produced in the analysis of work diaries.

Participatory data analysis workshop

Participants were invited to a data analysis workshop in March 2011. Seven participants attended; the remainder could not attend due to work commitments. The purpose of the workshop was to introduce selections of the data to the participants and to work with them to understand this data using CHAT. Although not an application of Developmental Work Research (Engeström 2007b), the research team's intention was to do more than seek respondent validation of their interpretations but rather to extend the analysis further by attempting to bring participants' insights into articulation. Selectively transcribed episodes from this workshop were analysed using MCA with a particular focus on how the categories (the ten job dimensions) were being built in participants' interactions.

The Work of Teacher Education

The ten job dimensions and the balance of working time

By focusing our analytic attention on the rules, the community and the division of labour, we were able to generate some simple, descriptive statistics about the work of the teacher educators in our sample. The average number of hours worked each week was 49, ranging from 32 to 71 hours, with seven participants (over half the sample) completing in excess of 45 hours work. Primary teacher educators worked on average for 51 hours during the week; secondary educators worked 48 hours. Overall, across the job dimensions and in relation to the sample as a whole, no relationship could be inferred between the number of hours worked and the geographical locations of participants, the type of employing institution or their length of service.

Table 3.2 provides the means and standard deviations for the hours attributed to the job dimensions that were in evidence during the week recorded in May 2010.

Table 3.2 Job dimensions (in hours) May 2010: Descending means and standard deviations

Work of teacher education: Job dimensions	N	Minimum	Maximum	Mean	Std. deviation
Relationship maintenance	13	3.0	31.0	13.192	6.9986
Marking	13	0.0	28.5	7.115	8.5736
Tutoring an individual student	13	0.0	30.0	6.500	7.9373
Working with a group of students	13	0.0	16.5	6.385	6.6525
Research	13	0.0	23.5	5.923	8.6671
Course management	13	0.5	15.0	5.192	4.1660
External examination at another institution	13	0.0	19.5	1.500	5.4083
Examination at own institution	13	0.0	18.0	1.423	4.9827
Professional development	13	0.0	11.5	1.077	3.1678
Personnel activities	13	0.0	5.0	0.615	1.4456

The job dimension on which the greatest number of hours was expended is *relationship maintenance*. In the case of *relationship maintenance* (mean, 13.192; SD, 6.9986), there is less variation in the number of hours worked than those spent on *research*, for example, where the standard deviation (8.6671) is higher than the accompanying mean (5.923). To exemplify this in terms of the data generated, seven participants (or 54 per cent of the sample) carried out zero hours of *research*, whereas everyone undertook a measure of *relationship maintenance*. For one person this amounted to only 3 hours; for everyone else, however, 8.5 hours (equivalent to more hours than might be prescribed as constituting an average working day) was the minimum time allocated. Of the twelve participants remaining, eleven spent between 8.5 and 19 hours on *relationship maintenance* during the week, with one further individual expending an outlying 31 hours on this activity.

In spite of conventional expectations across higher education, only six out of thirteen participants undertook any *research*. According to the results set out in Table 3.1, it may be possible to consider as 'customary', or as 'defining', those dimensions of the teacher educator's job which accounted, on average, for 5 or more hours of effort during the week (*relationship maintenance*; *marking*; *tutoring an individual student*; *working with a group of students*; *research*; *course management*). Of these dimensions, *research* was most often omitted within individuals' profiles. Indeed, were it not for two participants who undertook 20.5 and 23.5 hours of *research*, the latter could hardly be categorized as being a dimension of the teacher educator's work, as it might be classified according to the mean values in Table 3.2.

Table 3.3 provides the means and standard deviations for the hours attributed to the job dimensions in evidence during the week recorded in October 2010. When compared with the results in week 1, a number of similarities and differences become apparent. The most obvious difference is that a much greater number of hours was expended in October on *working with a group of students*, as we expected given the time of year and the point in ITE courses. The most apparent similarity is the number of hours spent on *relationship maintenance*.

Table 3.3 Job dimensions (in hours) October 2010: Descending means and standard deviations

Work of teacher education: Job dimensions	N	Minimum	Maximum	Mean	Std. Deviation
Working with a group of students	12	1.5	36.5	18.458	12.0632
Relationship maintenance	12	3.0	42.5	16.500	11.1049
Tutoring an individual student	12	0.0	17.5	4.625	5.0728
Course management	12	0.0	14.0	2.958	4.4694
Research	12	0.0	14.0	2.917	5.1027
Marking	12	0.0	9.0	2.708	2.9190
Professional development	12	0.0	7.5	0.875	2.1755
Personnel activities	12	0.0	5.0	0.417	1.4434
External examination at another institution	12	0.0	0.0	0.000	0.0000
Examination at own institution	12	0.0	0.0	0.000	0.0000

In order to compare the mean scores for the two groups, 6 months apart in time, a paired samples t-test was carried out. In the event, only one significant difference was revealed by the test: the increase in the number of hours spent working with groups of students ($t = -3.640$, $p < 0.004$). The importance of this finding to the results in general is in suggesting that the changes in the remaining mean scores are not large enough or consistent enough to refute the null hypothesis, which implies that for these dimensions of the job at least there was no measurable difference in the two weeks selected.

As comment-worthy as the rise in hours undertaken by the teacher educators in *working with a group of students* may prove to be, it is still the case that *relationship maintenance* accounted for both the highest maximum individual allocation of hours, and the highest minimum. For this sample of teacher educators, *relationship maintenance* appears to be the prevailing and defining characteristic of their work.

What is relationship maintenance?

In our observations of twelve participants, we identified numerous examples of *relationship maintenance* in all but two cases. The widespread nature of this job dimension was unsurprising given the analysis of work diary data and the observation data was therefore both confirmatory and explanatory. Superficially, the tasks underlying *relationship maintenance* could appear to be, in part, general administrative work: making and receiving telephone calls; writing and reading emails; writing letters; talking to a student, colleagues at the university and in schools. And all unrelated to one of the other job dimensions such as *tutoring an individual student*, for example, where the focus was either on academic progress or lesson observation. On closer analysis of the work diaries, however, and through observation, we found that the object of this communicative activity was in fact aimed at maintaining relationships with students, colleagues in schools and at the university. The majority of this work came under the broad heading of 'partnership'. Indeed, even when the focus was individual student health and well-being, the stress involved in crossing partnership boundaries between university and school was often the significant factor.

We observed our participants writing and responding to emails from student teachers as early as 7.30 a.m. (Natalie) and one reported staying at work the evening prior to the observation to 9.45 p.m. to clear such an email backlog (Duncan). Joyce spoke about the usefulness of a Bluetooth connection in her car so that she could make and receive such phone calls 'on the move' between school visits. These phone calls were often from or about student teachers under stress – absent from school or barely sustaining their attendance. In one case, that of Anne, 90 minutes on the day observed was taken up with dealing with one student who had absented herself from school and whose mentor, senior school staff and university link tutor were all concerned and/or angry. Anne's *relationship maintenance* activity involved voice mail messages to the student (in bed, asleep, when she called) and the school's senior staff (teaching when Anne called); writing long, carefully worded emails when telephone calls weren't possible; answering telephone calls that respond to voice messages; informal conversations with concerned university colleagues and a 40 minute meeting with the student teacher herself. In another case, Joyce made a home visit to a student teacher signed off sick with stress, a visit that took 1 hour including travelling time. Email was an important channel for *relationship maintenance* and participants were observed being highly responsive. In several cases, participants used audible signals on their computer to announce an email's arrival and one, Moira, had turned up the volume and was observed to be hyper-responsive to a high volume of email. During a short lunch break at her desk, Moira wrote four emails while simultaneously eating and drinking and also answered two telephone calls. During her attendance at a meeting lasting just over an hour, she received nine emails requiring the sort of work we are describing as *relationship maintenance*.

We also observed *relationship maintenance* built in to how individuals and institutions acted together at a strategic level. Daisy spent 10 minutes of a meeting with the school placement coordinator working out which student teachers could be sent to which schools as mentors had very specific criteria for the student teachers they would accept. One secondary science mentor, for example, strongly implied that he only wished to work with male students of Pakistani heritage backgrounds and another mentor in a private, single-sex, religious school would only take female students observant of that religion. Daisy's institution was in a geographic area where there was fierce competition for school placements among four HEIs so a level of *relationship maintenance* that took into account the preferences of individual mentors was deemed necessary. The two exceptions to *relationship maintenance* being observed during our fieldwork were Jo and Michelle. Jo taught a whole morning and part-afternoon session during our observation and her activities around this were preparatory. Michelle was observed visiting schools but not to observe students she knew. Michelle's university (for financial reasons, it had said) had abandoned subject- and phase-specific visiting and Michelle, as a secondary geography specialist, was observed visiting primary schools.

In the participatory data analysis workshop, Jo commented that when feeling vulnerable as a new researcher, it was sometimes tempting to devote more time than you should to tasks one you know you are good at, usually having been good at them in school: building, maintaining and repairing relationships. This comment produced a mixed response from the participants. It was clear, however, that good relationships (with students, colleagues and schools) were explicitly recognized as a priority by all participants – in interview, during observation and in participatory data analysis – as being key performance indicators under most evaluation, quality assurance and inspection regimes.

Teacher educators' talking about their work

The interviews elicited the teacher educators' accounts of a diverse set of practices and material conditions. Their teaching loads, office space, resources, contracts and so on were impacted by both local institutional and national policy-level tensions concerned with teaching in HEI (and in FE, in two cases) as well as the accountability, quality assurance and regulatory constraints associated with teacher education policy in the two countries. By their own accounts, this sample of teacher educators worked hard and was successful. They spoke about multiple transition points in their professional lives and represented these transitions as 'new challenges'. A great deal of the reward they reported from their work was from what they described as the personal and 'socially transformative' nature of their teaching – the success of the individual student in becoming a teacher and the year-on-year 'production' of new teachers for the profession, as well as, at times, the social mobility a teaching job might afford some students. Research did not consistently figure (or, in some cases, *ever* figure) in their accounts of their motivations to become teacher educators or in talking about their work. For some, it was not a contractual requirement; for others, it was merely a desirable 'extra'; for others again, it was deemed important by their institutions but they were given little or no guidance as to how to develop it. Through attributing phrases such as 'socially important' and 'a real buzz' to their work, and substantiating these attributions through personal narratives, the teacher educators in our sample conveyed both the pleasure they derived from working with student teachers and what they saw as the transformative project of teacher education.

Joyce, for example, directly linked her work to widening access to higher education and improving social mobility and talked about research she had started on the topic but abandoned due to time constraints. Teaching was also described as 'high-octane' and sometimes this was explained as a consequence of the need they felt to demonstrate exemplary practice and be a 'role model'. All of our sample responded very positively to our question about how they felt about their work as a teacher educator and connected their responses directly to their work with student teachers face-to-face. Three of the four participants with most experience (all based in England) were regretful about what they saw as policy-dictated changes in their roles and the new importance of what Martha described as 'a mainly quality assurance' function – ensuring partnership arrangements with schools 'ran smoothly', that mentors and students were 'satisfied' and did not complain, presenting a face of 'high quality provision' to Ofsted. What they actually taught, some felt, was no longer so important.

The teacher educators saw their work changing over time. For those relatively new to the job (with less than 6 years experience), this was most often accounted for in relation to research and scholarship. Joyce, for example, articulated her awareness of identity shifts, asking herself the question, '*Am I an academic?*' Jo, as we noted, was unusual for the amount of time she allocated to research so it was interesting she still asked herself this question. Michelle spoke about her transition into the Education department of a Scottish university using the metaphor of a game: 'it's a new game and you need to learn the rules of that game, and the rules quite often change'. She reported the conditions of her probationary period being changed to raise the stakes from completing a master's degree to having 'REF-able' publications. Along with all of her colleagues, she had been publicly 'colour coded' by the management of her department to indicate current research activity and future potential. Michelle was 'green', the lowest point on this scale. Unsurprisingly, perhaps, she described writing for publication as 'keeping the wolf from the door'. The arbitrary nature of this game was also visible to Michelle and to Jo: they may work hard and produce publications but there was still no guarantee they would be of sufficiently high quality to be entered in the REF and to be counted as 'research active'.

Teacher educators who had more experience often spoke about the ways they had had to adapt to the changes within their own institutions. Brendan, for example, talked about the developmental trajectory of the teacher educator as not being linear; he saw his own development as contingent and reversible, saying, 'as soon as you get reconciled to, you know, what you're doing, they change everything.... So you either revalidate the degree that you're working on, or they drop your specialism, or they reorganise the department that you're working in.... So it never quite sort of flows from one end to the other'. The overall impression was of a group of people who were good at navigating the transitions of a life course, highly flexible, responsive to demand and adaptive to new situations.

Concluding comments

The research on school-based teacher educators' (mentors') work suggests that their social support and practical feedback on immediate teaching situations is highly valued by student teachers. This line of research also suggests that the focus of the mentoring relationship can sometimes be on competence against what might be fairly narrow or even idiosyncratic criteria. The literature on the interactions between school-based and HEI-based teacher educators and student teachers – often described as a triadic relationship – also suggests that a discourse of civility mediates the possibilities for teacher learning, possibilities that are constrained by contextually necessary but sometimes extreme levels of tact and diplomacy. In these circumstances, open dialogue and critical debate on matters of pedagogy are difficult to achieve for reasons to do with social structures of power but also with local cultures. Our research in the WoTE project suggested that the defining characteristic of the HEI-based teacher educators in our sample was *relationship maintenance* – communicative activity required to keep the fragile networks of relationships within ITE partnerships in England on an even keel and capable of demonstrating compliance or even 'outstanding' performance in a competitive, quasi-market of teacher education 'providers'.

Taken together, the potential for the full development of teachers in the English model of ITE is constrained by the work that it is possible for school-based mentors and HEI-based tutors to do within the system. Moreover, we believe that it is the division of labour between academic workers in HEI Education departments as well as the division of labour between HEI-based and school-based workers that is at issue.

In the next chapter, we return to the WoTE study and specifically to the work of four women employed as HEI-based teacher educators to provide a rich and detailed sense of the kinds of work that are possible within current configurations of ITE in England. For international readers, especially in countries like the United States and some parts of continental Europe, where tenure track and highly professionalized higher education career structures exist, the narratives we present of a 'day in the life' of a teacher educator may or may not be surprising. In England, our experience is that when we have shared these narratives with colleagues and at conferences, they are found to be recognizable while at the same time being predictable and disturbing.

4

Teacher Educators at Work: Narratives of Experience

The four women whose work is represented in this chapter were all part of the original sample of HEI-based teacher educators in the WoTE study. Daisy, Anne, Natalie and Sally worked in different types of HEIs around England; two working almost exclusively on secondary ITE programmes, one working in primary ITE and one, Sally, increasingly across both phases. At the time of the first stage of the research in 2010–2011, all four had the title of Lecturer in Education, with Sally (like Joyce) being unusual in that she worked in a higher education unit within a further education college. This contractual situation meant that all but two of the complete WoTE sample – and three of the four women whose stories we tell here – were on standard academic (teaching and research) contracts in English HEIs. They were expected to do research and, if they ever sought promotion to senior lecturer (associate professor), they would be expected to demonstrate research achievements.

In the process of generating data for the first stage of the study, we interviewed Daisy, Anne, Natalie and Sally at two points in the year – near the beginning and towards the end. They completed work diaries, as we explained in the previous chapter. We observed them for whole days at their places of work; we asked them to invite us to what they would consider a 'typical' working day for the time of year (of course, we cannot be certain these days were typical but have trusted our participants and taken their selections at face value). They also attended our participatory data analysis workshop at the end of the project. At the end of this first stage, we invited those who attended our participatory data analysis workshop to continue their relationship with us over the following year – to allow us to visit them again at work and to continue the conversations we had started. Five women accepted our invitation – including the four who are the focus of this chapter. To this extent, the narratives that follow are those of a self-selecting group and also a subset of a purposive rather than a representative sample.

In developing these narratives, we draw on the data we have generated, some of it from an ethnographic perspective (Green & Bloome 1997, Heath & Street 2007). We do not claim to have produced anything like an ethnography *per se* but do claim some engagement with ethnographic practice. Likewise, our representation and analysis of the data have been guided by what Paul Willis has called 'the ethnographic imagination' (Willis 2000): the data does not 'speak for itself'; it is not raw or unmediated. Rather, it has been shaped by our attempts to understand other people's lived experience through our own. Deborah Britzman (1991) put it like this: 'it is for researchers to narrate and interpret the words of others and render their own process of understanding' (p. 51). That was our goal in writing this chapter and the one that follows.

In presenting the chapter in this way, we realize we are running the risk of presenting something that critics may describe as 'mere stories' and perhaps 'sob stories' at that. We do not regard narrative as a genre as trivial nor do we see it as naively atheoretical. Narrative is just as – and perhaps more than – capable of conveying abstract concepts and developing theory as more obviously theoretically mediated and 'thematically organized' qualitative analyses of lived experience, as narrative theorists, psychologists and ethnographers have long claimed (e.g. Britzman 1991, Bruner 1986, Walkerdine 1988). Furthermore, as Calhoun (1994) put it:

> One of the drawbacks to thinking in terms of such binary oppositions as general theory versus narrative is that we are not encouraged to examine the questions of whether the strategies may complement each other or whether there are analytic problems that may call for one more than the other. (p. 868)

Our view is that in our efforts to capture and represent the lived experience of the teacher educators at work, these narrative accounts will help us to analyse the concrete details and material conditions within which teacher education as a form of academic labour is produced. The theoretically driven analysis that follows in Chapter 5 picks up on our earlier discussion of the history and politics of teacher education as well as the concept of academic capitalism that we introduced in the previous chapter and the multiple forms of data generated with the whole sample. By delaying the 'big theory' we know that we are violating what Foley (2002) called a 'sacred convention of scientific realist narratives' – the parallel running of 'theoretical commentary' and 'thick description' (p. 481). Rather than seeing this violation as an issue, we view our challenge instead as one of not sentimentalizing the teacher educators in these narratives and of seeking to draw out the contradictions and tensions in their stories so as to reveal more clearly the nature of the problem that is the object of our research.

Teacher educators at work

Daisy

Lowtown is in the north of England, a once thriving city with a proud industrial heritage, the centre of which has now been hollowed-out by successive economic crises. A tree grows from the roof of a derelict cinema in the main square and the shops are now a mixture of pawnbrokers and fast-food outlets, Cash Converters and Chicken Cottages. Up on the hill, the local university looks down at the city centre, surrounded by terraced houses that are now occupied mainly by undergraduate students. Nearby, a solid, Victorian, brick building provides a contrast with the university's glass and concrete structures. It was once the local day training college and is now part of a very large and entrepreneurial further education college that has a centre for higher education. There, in an extension to the college completed in the 1970s, Daisy works as head of the secondary teacher education programme and lead tutor for science.

Arriving at her desk by 8 a.m., Daisy spends 10 minutes working through emails. There are concerns from her colleagues about the poor behaviour of student teachers in a subject knowledge enhancement course; messages about external examiners and questions about the process of bidding for taught degree-awarding powers (the college wants to be able to award its own degrees). She makes a phone call to order catering for a meeting. A colleague puts his head around the door to say hello and ask about Daisy's daughter, who will undergo major surgery the following day.

Her conversation with a colleague turns to workload: as a higher education lecturer, she is contracted to teach 777 hours per academic year; this compares to 850 hours for her colleagues who teach only in the further education college and 550 hours for her friends and at the university next door. Later, prompted by more emails, Daisy talks about the process for applying for degree-awarding powers; it is important to the college management. One of the criteria for being given these powers is that academic staff become external examiners at other institutions. Daisy says the college encourages them to become examiners but they then either must give their examining fee to the college or take a day's leave to do the work. These arrangements make it difficult for both the institution and the individuals to achieve their goals.

Just after 9 a.m., Daisy leaves for a school visit, arriving at the school at 9.45 a.m. On the journey, she passes an enormous, empty office building formerly occupied by a bank that was restructured following the 2008 global financial crisis. Birds are nesting in the cracked windows and graffiti covers the ground floor walls. The school visit is to observe a PGCE secondary science student who is 2 weeks into her first school placement. The lesson begins and Daisy is ready at a bench in the science lab with various forms and extracts from handbooks. The lesson includes a practical activity and the children move around noisily collecting items and assembling the experiment. Daisy is writing a running record of the lesson, very neatly, onto a lesson observation form. She moves only once to interact with the children and then returns to the bench to continue writing the running record. She writes 'Don't allow interruptions. Ensure clear boundaries – prevents fragmentation'.

As the lesson ends, Daisy starts writing a 'General Comments Form' about the lesson. The form is carbonated in triplicate: white for the student teacher; yellow for the mentor teacher; pink for Daisy herself. The children start to pack up and Daisy is still writing, rushing to fill in the boxes.

At break time, Daisy feeds back to the student teacher in the science lab with the mentor present but largely silent. The mentor has also completed some observation forms but the conversation is led by Daisy with occasional, short responses from the student teacher. Daisy begins by reading through her completed observation form. She asks the student teacher how she felt (as a biologist) teaching physics. The student teacher comments that the subject knowledge enhancement course she had attended really helped her. Questions and answers continue. The break ends and the mentor has to rush to teach. Daisy and the student teacher move to continue the conversation in a science prep room. Daisy checks the student's teaching files – a large lever-arch file full of planning, resources and college forms.

Daisy continues to complete paperwork as she talks. By now, she has completed a lesson observation form, a General Comments Form, a Link Tutor Visit Form and followed a Link Tutor Discussion Prompt Sheet. Prompted by the latter, she asks the student teacher questions: 'are you collecting evidence? You need to collect evidence. You've got some evidence here, haven't you?' And pointing to parts of the trainee's teaching file, 'These forms are evidence.'

Daisy drives back to the college, arriving at 12.20 p.m. There is more traffic on the way back into the city. She buys a sandwich from the reception coffee bar, dodging 14-year-olds as they hustle for chocolate bars and dash to their vocational education classes. She eats the sandwich in her office, taking two phone calls, one of which is about the difficulty of maintaining student records when Daisy's college data management system (designed for FE students) doesn't have fields for essential items of data for the HEI students.

Early in the afternoon, Daisy, as head of secondary teacher education, sees a 'naughty' student who has been reported for misbehaving in a subject knowledge enhancement course. He is in his mid-twenties, a pharmacy graduate from the university next door; a young, Pakistani-heritage man with a cheerful demeanour and colourful trainers. He seems oblivious to there being any concerns.

This meeting is rapidly followed by one between Daisy, as head of secondary teacher education, and the overall head of teacher education at the college. The agenda is wide ranging: the college's contribution to the local science festival (Daisy suggests something on female physicists and radioactivity); the self-evaluation document (SED) for Ofsted inspection purposes; the college's new mission statement and, in passing, the difference between 'ITT' (Initial Teacher Training) and 'ITE' (Initial Teacher Education) and whether it is a meaningful difference.

The discussion about the Ofsted SED focuses on data and what counts as data. In particular, the head of teacher education picks up on the government's advice not to 'over-rely' on Ofsted data. Daisy comments on the range of data sources she and her colleagues draw on for SED purposes; in preparing the SED she has referred to 168 separate documents. An important source of information is the 'CCRs' (Course Continuation Reviews), evaluation documents required by the university that currently awards the college's qualifications. The agenda turns to staff expenses (some lecturers aren't completing the forms properly); the use of the Harvard referencing system in academic assignments ('everybody in the secondary team needs to use the same system' says the head of teacher education, 'I'm flabbergasted they don't') and peer observation of teaching as part of the appraisal process. The final item on the agenda is staff taking master's degrees at the college. The head of teacher education asks whether anyone in the secondary team is interested in doing a master's degree: 'this is the last year they'll get their fees back'.

Daisy walks to another part of the college for a meeting with the School Partnership Coordinator, who chairs the Partnership Committee and oversees the placement of students in schools. As lead tutor for secondary science, she has thirty-nine student teachers to place for the second school experience with only seventeen places offered by schools thus far. When the meeting begins, they talk first about a meeting of the partnership committee and organizational issues. Who will set up the catering? Who will take minutes? One agenda item for the partnership committee is a 'student agreement' – a document picked up from one of the 'London ITT providers' that sets out expectations (behavioural as well as pedagogical) of student teachers (e.g. handing in assignments on time; arriving at school punctually). Daisy says that the London institution makes every student teacher sign such an agreement. As we look over, it looks to us like a behaviour contract that some schools use with 'challenging' pupils.

They continue to talk about mentor training; e-portfolio systems for capturing 'student progression data' and developing criteria for the placement of students in schools. They note that, as an institution, they have 'guidance … but not criteria … why should you be placed close to your home just because you don't have a car'. They discuss individual student teachers: the partnership coordinator says, about one case in particular, 'another reason why the school doesn't want to keep her is that she is self-mutilating and they didn't think that was a good role model'.

As the meeting develops, it becomes clear that placing student teachers is a very complicated affair. Mr Khan, a head of science and mentor in a secondary school, will only accept Pakistani-heritage male student teachers; he will not accept female student teachers or white student teachers. Daisy's college works with independent schools as well as state schools and has good links with a local, private Muslim school. This school insists that any Asian female student teacher placed there wear the headscarf (niqab), whether or not they usually do. For female Muslim student teachers that do not normally wear the headscarf, this requirement is presented to them by the college as 'conforming to the dress code of the school'. A sentence to that effect has been inserted in the information given to all students in their pre-course information.

Daisy returns to her office at 3 p.m. and continues to work at her desk, responding to emails and making phone calls. She then goes for a meeting with a colleague who is in charge of scheduling classes and allocating rooms for the whole college.

Daisy is ensuring that there are adequate rooms for secondary PGCE students and that no rooms are booked that aren't used. The timetabler says: 'We need to tighten up.' Daisy agrees. The meeting ends at 4 p.m. and Daisy returns to her office.

Daisy continues to follow up today's meetings in emails to her colleagues who need to know outcomes and action points. She goes to pick up some photocopying and on the way bumps into a PGCE student who has dropped by after school, with his young daughter. She talks to the little girl and to her father, who has come in for some advice. The father looks tired. They talk about school and the classes he's teaching. She spends some more time working at her desk and about 5 p.m. closes her computer down and packs up ready to leave and go home. She won't be coming in for the next 2 days. She will accompany her daughter to hospital tomorrow and stay for the operation and through the early stages of recovery.

Next week, she will begin teaching in the evening on master's-level CPD courses for local teachers. She is down to teach action research methods, something she is both looking forward to and dreading. Daisy tells us she doesn't have a master's degree herself; she started one but gave up due to time pressure. At times, she says, she feels like a fraud: she has never done any action research herself, again citing lack of time. She knows research is a good thing, though, believes in it, wants to do it. But it is also something that she sees as out of reach if she also wishes to lead a secondary teacher education programme that is deemed 'outstanding' by Ofsted.

Anne

Anne works in an 'old' university, established in the nineteenth century and now based on several campuses in the town of Piltsfield. The university has been judged to be one of the ten most research-intensive universities in the UK. The campus where Anne works is located on the site of a former training college that, in the late 1980s, had amalgamated with the university. Piltsfield itself is a commercial centre in the south of England, principally for information technology and insurance businesses.

Anne took up her current post as a Lecturer in Education just this year. For a year before that, she had worked in the department on a part-time basis coordinating the Student Associate Scheme and then running the Subject Knowledge Enhancement course. Recently, due to staffing problems, Anne was asked to 'act up' to become the PGCE Course Leader for Secondary Science; she is the only full-time science tutor in her department, coordinating the work of three part-time colleagues.

It is a Thursday and at about 7.30 a.m., Anne arrives in her office. In this small room she has a computer and printer as well as a range of professional texts and a few issues of academic journals. There are also more than ten 'Thank You' cards on the shelves. All of the science tutors are together on this floor along with teaching labs and prep rooms. There is also a communal space where staff can take breaks and socialize. Anne begins her day reading emails and taking a phone call from a school about a 'wobbly trainee'. Like her colleagues, she always uses the word 'trainee' rather than 'student'. She tells us that the trainee has been unwell but is also prone to anxiety and the school has recently become concerned about her anxiety levels in triggering another bout of illness. The school wanted to check that it was alright to reduce the trainee's timetable and Anne tells them it is but to involve the trainee in this decision making. This year she has set up a small 'special group' that comprises the 'at-risk trainees' in the hope that they can offer each other mutual support. Anne is currently the tutor for six PGCE trainees, two master's students and leads the course for the entire cohort of thirty-nine trainees plus supervising seven trainees on what was then the university's employment-based route, the Graduate Teacher Programme (GTP).

Anne has been involved with colleagues in the Caribbean on a CPD project that aims, through the use of Assessment for Learning, 'to shift teachers away from didactic teaching styles', she says. This was an important initiative for the university and could possibly lead to more contracts and financial reward for the department. Anne hopes to produce a paper from this project and today, being a quiet day, she had earmarked to work on this. However, an email from a professional tutor about a trainee who has absented herself from school needs to be dealt with. This is not uncommon, as she says, as 'things come along to fill the day up'.

A colleague, Will, enters Anne's office to ask about Jo, the missing trainee; he had arranged for her to come to the department at 9 a.m. but she hadn't appeared yet. They both wonder about her whereabouts, they are also concerned about her 'mental state' and about how unsupportive the school is being. Will and Anne then go off to the team room to make coffee and with the PGCE coordinator they talk about the previous night when the science trainees were in the department for a twilight session, more a pastoral than academic event. Anne says its purpose was 'to look into their eyes and make sure everything is OK'. When Anne returns to her office she phones Jo, leaving a message on her voicemail trying not to sound annoyed about her failure to show and making sure she knows that Anne is available all day for a chat. Anne tells us that mentors can be less than supportive especially with such trainees; they can 'be less than generous' she says.

At 9.45 a.m. Jo surfaces and phones Anne. She has just woken up, she says, and they arrange a time to meet later. Anne then turns her attention to dealing with emails. She doesn't stop typing for 20 minutes or so. One email, to Jo's mentor, takes a particularly long time to compose because of confidentiality. Anne has to be careful what she reveals in an email but she also needs to ensure that the school 'gets the right message'. Anne continues to respond to emails for a further 15 minutes until Bev, another colleague who runs the primary course, enters to talk about the department's move to another site in the town. Although the move will mean that the Education Department will have a single building to itself, science will actually end up with less space and their dedicated technicians will be shared amongst the whole department. Anne and Bev discuss the lack of car parking space at the new site and the problems this might cause for mentors attending meetings; they are worried that this could impact upon mentor attendance. They discuss the possibility of encouraging staff to work more at home to free-up parking spaces and Anne asks Bev to bring this up at the Head of Department's forum. They both go into one of the main prep rooms to talk further with a technician about moving everything.

Anne returns to her office at 10.30 a.m. and Bev soon returns because she had forgotten to ask about GTP trainees, specifically, she wants to know 'what's the pay back for taking GTP trainees on her course?' At the university, GTP trainees have always been included in the secondary PGCE teaching sessions but not primary ones. Anne tells Bev that she uses the money for teaching the GTP students to pay sessional tutors. But as they agree, the problem is that more trainees just means more marking. Also GTP trainees are visited twice as many times a year than the PGCE trainees. They then talk about how to replace the retiring primary science tutor. Anne says that the secondary team have spare capacity – a colleague has returned earlier than expected from a period of ill health and the person, Will, who covered this is now 'surplus'. Bev wonders if secondary tutors have the expertise to do primary work but Anne reassures her that Will is both keen and able. Bev seems to be more convinced by this and they discuss what sorts of role Will might have on the primary programme. Anne is keen to keep Will on her team and thinks giving him some primary work will help her to do this. The PGCE coordinator then pops her head in to ask about Jo and also about a potential applicant to the subject knowledge enhancement course.

Anne makes a phone call to her research mentor, the deputy director of research, who will also be her PhD supervisor. She asks whether she needs to submit the paper in order to get funding from the university to attend the conference in the Caribbean in February. When she is told that she does, Anne asks if he will review the paper for her. Having lost time to work on the paper today, she is worried that she won't get it done in time, she is right up against the deadline for submission.

At 11 a.m., Anne meets the ITT leader, the PGCE coordinator and the quality assurance administrator to discuss the return to the course of a trainee who suspended his PGCE course. We sit and observe in what is a small meeting room. They draw up a plan of action for the return of the trainee to school. This meeting lasts for 30 minutes and then Anne meets with the ITT leader for a further 15 minutes to talk about issues related to another school where the professional tutor has not been supporting a mentor who is struggling with another 'wobbly' trainee. The two colleagues agree upon a course of action that each will pursue. At 11.45 a.m., Anne returns to her office to compose a long email to the professional tutor, the mentor and the tutor about the returning trainee. She tells us that such trainees cause extra work, lots of emails and phone calls have to be made. At midday another colleague arrives for a brief meeting about the organization of January's science education conference that Anne is helping to organize at the university. Fifteen minutes later Anne starts to write up the notes of the previous night's twilight meeting that she will email out to all trainees, including the couple that did not attend. She says that her colleagues with smaller cohorts can just meet informally in the pub to catch up rather than have to organize special meetings and then write up notes for those who did not attend, 'with 39 you just can't do that', she says.

At 12.25 p.m., Jo arrives and there is a lengthy meeting. During the meeting, Jo cries and Anne tries to persuade her to at least complete the term in school even if she then decided to suspend her studies. After this meeting, Anne says that she will now contact Jo's tutor to make arrangements for further support for the last 2 weeks of the term. Anne then goes off to a session about supervising master's students where a sandwich lunch is provided. During this meeting, Anne gets out her laptop and catches up on some emails that arrived during her meeting with Jo. She deals with an email from Jo's mentor; Anne informs the mentor that the university will take the lead in devising a programme of support for Jo. For part of the session, tutors are supposed to look at examples of dissertations but, like the other tutors on Anne's table, she does not engage with this task. She says 'it is difficult to assess quality so quickly'. However, Anne says that at least she now knows who she can ask to help her with masters' work in the future. After the meeting Anne takes four cakes from the meeting upstairs for Will and the three technicians. She also briefly talks to Will about how tutors will 'bolster' the support for Jo and they briefly chat about the possibility of him doing some work on the primary programme.

At 2.45 p.m. Anne returns to her office to deal with more emails and to make a phone call to Jo's professional tutor but they were unavailable so she asks, again unsuccessfully, to speak to the mentor. She leaves a message to let the school know that Jo will be returning and that she will contact the professional tutor and mentor by email to map out what support is being offered. She gets chance to have a chat with the other science trainee and questions him about the atmosphere there. It is a tricky conversation that Anne has some concerns about. 'Did she say too much to the trainee?,' she ponders. She did ascertain that things had got quite negative for Jo there. To follow up and to smooth the waters for Jo's return, Anne carefully crafts an email to the school. She says that it is difficult to do this with an email and this is why she tried to phone initially. She copies the trainee's university tutor into the email too, another long message.

At 3 p.m. Anne picks up material for a Science, Technology, Engineering and Mathematics meeting tomorrow at another university, leaves her office to drop this in her car and then walks over to a research methods seminar run by her research mentor. These seminars are held weekly and relate to teaching and learning or research methods or involve presentations of people's research. Anne says that she will use her tablet computer to check emails and work on her laptop on the train tonight. But she does also check emails during the seminar. Anne misses questions at the end because she has to leave at 3.40 p.m. to catch her train. The train travels north, Anne responding to emails on her tablet as the evening comes. Then she starts marking.

Natalie

Saxborough, home to the university where Natalie works, is a market town in the south-east of England. The institution was awarded its university status in 1992, one of the large number of former polytechnics that became universities that year. Overall, the university is very new and modern in design and the campus itself forms part of the community; planning for it was only allowed if the university also built a community centre.

Natalie is a relatively new teacher educator and doesn't see herself as having much experience. In her own words she came into teacher education accidentally, characteristic of her whole career path from doctoral student in mathematics, to unqualified teacher, to banker, to primary school teacher via the GTP route into teaching and finally to HEI-based teacher educator. She found moving from a small primary school to a large university campus challenging. Initially she felt 'out of place and de-skilled' and found her university 'an odd place to work', she tells us. However, she found her immediate colleagues helpful and supportive; the team of people she works with is close knit. Although she values this highly, she has found that in contrast to being a teacher, where she felt much more able to work at her own pace, she has found working as a team can slow her down. On the upside, she notes that working with others makes her question her own thinking and practice and she recognizes that she enjoys that.

Natalie works on the BEd and PGCE primary programmes, although she does some teaching on other programmes such as the BA Educational Studies course and a specialist mathematics teachers' course. Natalie is the only person in the primary mathematics ITE team at Saxborough University with degrees in mathematics and so she has been given the role of the primary mathematics coordinator, leading a team of four who work across programme. Although Natalie says she enjoys her work on the whole, the large number of students on the primary BEd course (140 students each year) means that she isn't able to get to know the students and she tells us she doesn't like how this feels.

Natalie routinely arrives at her desk by 8 a.m., although frequently she might arrive earlier to miss the traffic but also to prepare for teaching. She works in a large, open-plan office with nine colleagues who all also work in ITE and, observing, we note the space. The office has four pods with four desks in each pod; each person has a desk in addition to a wardrobe-sized lockable cupboard. The other offices in the corridor are similarly arranged. Natalie's office appears to us fairly impersonal: there are no personal posters or photographs on display but she tells us she does keep a series of professional texts and other resources in her cupboard. The resources had been purchased from her own personal funds and so, to save money, she had put these resources together with a colleague to share the cost. 'It is difficult,' she volunteers, 'to get money back from the Department'. Natalie used to share this office with maths, English and science primary colleagues and, being new to ITE, she relished this as a space for learning from others. However, the leadership team had recently decided to reorganize, for reasons unbeknown to Natalie, and she now shares the office with a mixture of secondary and other subject colleagues. Professionally, she has little in common with these people and says she feels she learns less.

Arriving at work, she finds that her closest maths colleague, Paul, is already at work and she begins by switching on her computer to look at the university's virtual learning environment where she begins to amend some lesson-planning templates. At 8.30 a.m., we observe Natalie starting to check a PowerPoint presentation and she works with her own laptop linked to her desktop computer so that any changes are made to both versions and she can work on them anytime. She checks with her colleague if he is OK for his lecture at 9 a.m. for the first-year BEd on the theme of calculation.

Continuing to prepare the PowerPoint, Natalie dips into a department copy of a textbook for primary maths teachers. After several minutes she goes back to amending her PowerPoint, at the same time making notes on a copy of the handout. Beside her is a pack of self-made coloured cards, 4 cm × 8 cm in size, with simple calculations on them; these are to be used for a true/false quiz she will give her students.

Natalie then works on another PowerPoint for teaching she will be doing at the weekend. She flips between working on the two presentations from time to time. The planning for the weekend teaching prompts her to make a phone call to enquire about resources – strings of beads – that she thinks she will need and she follows this up by taking her own string of beads down to the technician's office one floor below to ask about getting some more beads as she is missing some – and talks about possible alternatives. There are three technicians who provide support to ITE staff. The weekend course is residential for the teachers and this will mean that Natalie won't get home until 4 p.m. on Sunday. She will be teaching at 9 a.m. on the Monday morning.

Returning to her office, Natalie continues to work on her presentation for the weekend. She searches on the internet for a suitable image of a ruler to paste into a slide and selects one image. When a colleague enters the office, we note that Natalie does not acknowledge her in any way and similarly, when another colleague arrives to place something on a desk. It seems as though they have all become used to the traffic.

At 9.55 a.m., Natalie gathers up her teaching materials and laptop and leaves for the teaching room; we follow. It is large and bright with a data projector, an interactive whiteboard, other movable whiteboards, tables and chairs. Academic staff do not generally have dedicated or even subject-specific teaching rooms and therefore Natalie comes in early to move the furniture around and set up equipment. She does this because she says 'you have to ask a porter two weeks in advance to do this for you and then they don't turn up'. Onto each desk she puts copies of the government's National Strategy Framework Literacy and Numeracy document and a few calculators also. She connects her laptop and props the door open as students begin to arrive.

Shortly after 10 a.m., the session (for BEd students) begins with Natalie asking students to jot down one thing gained from the morning's lecture and follows this up by asking some questions to find out what they had picked up. In all there are thirty-five students, just four men. Then she asks the students to write down different sums whose answers are always 10. Natalie does not use any of the students' names during her questioning as it is a BEd class and Natalie rarely gets to know them well. About 15 minutes later, a group of six students go to the front of the room and role-play a teaching scenario to the rest of the class. On the whiteboard, Natalie then works through a couple of subtractions to show the students how pupils might approach the bingo game she has planned. This is then followed by the true/false quiz using the cards she had made which both check the students' own mathematical understanding but also models an activity they might use. During the session, Natalie refers to her annotated handout from time to time.

About an hour into the session, they watch a video clip of a pupil doing mathematics under the guidance of a teacher. The clip lasts little more than 4 minutes and, as they watch it, the students refer to some partial transcripts of the teaching episode. At one point, Natalie stops the video to draw the students' attention to the differences between the mathematical skills adults have in comparison to those of a child. She then directs the students to try similar simple mathematical calculations using calculators. By 11.30 a.m., some students finish this task and Natalie refers them to a couple of particular pages of the course resources book to try some of the activities there and also to read a related article. She then puts up a PowerPoint slide to remind students about a school-based task that requires them to talk to teachers about some ideas in the classroom and she shows them a lesson-planning template that is matched to the QTS Standards. She then puts up another slide and uses it to set 'homework', which is a so-called Directed Task, as well as reminding students to complete their weekly reflective logs and the specified reading. In assessing the students' answers during the session, Natalie decides that National Strategy document is not needed to support the students' mathematical understanding.

Natalie deliberately finishes the activity 10 minutes early to go back to revisit a mathematical problem that the group had not managed to get onto in last week's session. They use whiteboards to show Natalie their answers. As the students do this task, Natalie leaves the room to go to a resources room where she collects two large bright yellow sponge dice. When she returns she uses these dice to model for the students how they could use a game in the classroom that helps teach the mathematical concept of place value.

At a couple of minutes before midday, the session finishes and the students leave in dribs and drabs. However, Natalie catches one student to talk to her about continual absences from the course. Natalie has found that it is necessary to 'come down hard' on such students, particularly in the first year, although at the same time recognizing that it is a stage they often start to feel overwhelmed. In her communication with this student, she is sensitive to this and attempts to sort out how she can catch up what has been missed.

After the student leaves, Natalie has lunch in the nearby community centre. At 12.50 p.m., she returns to the same teaching room and sets it up as before. She knows this group even less well than the morning group – a group of around thirty students (three men) – because it is normally taught by another colleague currently absent from work. The session begins just after 1 p.m. and Natalie runs it along very similar lines to the one in the morning. The group and paired tasks take about 10 minutes longer this afternoon and consequently there is less time at the end of the session to do the game with the dice. As before, Natalie reminds the group about tasks and the homework set. One student comments that she had tried out a Countdown game with her own daughter and Natalie remembers that she has a copy of a Countdown game on her laptop and provides her memory stick for the student to copy the game. Another student requests a copy, so Natalie gives her the memory stick too.

At about 4 p.m., Natalie returns to her office to meet with Paul and together they discuss the weekend course and finalize the session plans. Despite her teaching workload, Natalie tells us she has taken it upon herself to make a start as an educational.researcher by signing up to some research-related CPD. She is also exploring how she might track subject knowledge development with PGCE primary students to develop her own small research project. Around 5 p.m., Natalie leaves to attend a research-related CPD session on academic writing organized by her department, one of a series of 'twilight' sessions. When it ends at 6.30 p.m., the rush hour is over and Natalie has a relatively quick drive home.

Sally

Sally works in Mickleton, a large, multicultural city in the English midlands. Based on one campus, the University of Mickleton is a research university that has consistently been ranked among the top fifteen universities in the country in the various journalistic league tables. Sally joined Mickleton as a Lecturer in English Education in September 2008. Prior to this, she had been an English and Media Studies teacher in a secondary school during which time she had also studied for a master's in English Literature.

At Mickleton, she quickly began to teach on programmes other than the English secondary PGCE course for which she had been originally employed. Very soon she was asked to teach on the primary PGCE course, a foundation degree course and other BA courses in the Department of Education. This diversification, she says, has led to her job title of Lecturer in English Education evolving into Lecturer in Education. Sally has no experience of teaching of the primary phase and yet she increasingly does a lot of teaching on primary programmes. She tells us she wonders why she ever got the job in the first place.

Sally says some days are particularly heavy in terms of workload. For instance, she tells us she often finds herself teaching four 1.5-hour long sessions, each with thirty primary PGCE students. She says she feels overwhelmed with her teaching load at the same time as beginning to study for a PhD. On appointment, she was told she needed to become 'research active' and a PhD was an essential requirement. She is concerned that her 2-year review is coming up and she needs to publish two articles before the end of the academic year. Sally says she looks at her increasing and increasingly diverse teaching load and wonders how she will achieve this goal.

A single parent, Sally today arrived at 9.25 a.m., later than normal as she had to take her daughter to school. Her first move is to get a coffee in the department's staff room. There, we note that Sally quickly finds herself in a lengthy conversation with a colleague about a PGCE Professional Studies session on lesbian, gay, bisexual and transgender (LGBT) issues earlier in the week and about an LGBT group that Sally has set up to support and facilitate peer counselling for students. Sally then goes to her office in another part of the building. We see that it is a small room with a desk and chair and a single 'comfy' chair. It is dominated by a tent-like structure that Sally tells us she uses in her teaching to model how different social spaces can create different genres of linguistic interaction. There is also a computer, but no printer. The printer is in the corridor and shared by six other staff. She says she gets on well with the staff in the main office and so is able to get things printed there. Overall, the room is colourful, busy and lived-in.

Sally turns her computer on and spends time reading and responding to emails. She then picks up some PGCE students' coursework and starts marking it. She says she always has lots of marking. Printing off more students' work, Sally goes out into the corridor to collect it and then comes back in to start to write comments on it. In addition to the marginal comments, she also writes two paragraphs of feedback, including questions to prompt discussion. She prefers to write marginal comments rather than use 'track changes' as the assignment was a paired one and the two students will need the assignment on paper to look at together.

Sally says that sometimes her students can be uncritical. For example, in some recent teaching, she says, they had developed a superhero character along sexually stereotypical lines whereas she had wanted them to think about how to challenge such stereotypes with pupils. Sally says her 'professional pride' means that she spends a good deal of time giving feedback to individual students. It is important to model good practice and because it is really difficult to give good group feedback to a group of thirty-seven students, she says. If she doesn't get time during sessions, she says she also emails students to comment on their contributions. At 10.15 a.m. Sally leaves the room to collect some more printing and this, together with the work that she has put comments on, is put into a plastic envelope and stored for later. She then updates student records on her computer and shares the record with her course colleague.

Just after 11 a.m. Sally goes to the staff room for a coffee break and we follow. Sally talks to a colleague about a student who has been advised to seek counselling for anxiety and they discuss how they will facilitate this request. On returning to her office, she deals with a phone call about qualifications needed by an applicant for the PGCE course. She then walks to her colleague's office to clarify further the applicant's qualifications. On returning 5 minutes later, Sally phones another colleague about a spare theatre ticket for tonight's trip; Sally is taking her secondary PGCE students to see a play and one has had to drop out. Just before midday she looks at some PGCE application forms and then completes the related paperwork. The paperwork for each applicant is detailed and takes some time to complete, recording reasons for decisions against each criterion. She also completes her own records on her computer. This, she says, helps her to track applicants.

Mickleton's vice chancellor (VC) has recently stipulated that 95 per cent of postgraduate students must have at least a 2.1 honours degree. Sally says that this means that PGCE tutors like her might not be able to take some potentially excellent applicants. In one current dilemma, a Bengali-heritage student, who had a 2.2 honours degree but excellent potential as a teacher according to the application form and references, is probably going to have to be rejected in order to meet the VC's aspiration.

At 12.25 p.m., Sally joins a session being run by an outside speaker about teaching Shakespeare's *Hamlet*. When the session finishes, Sally gives the students some brief instructions for the afternoon session and then goes for lunch herself. She generally brings her own lunch as the catering facilities are poor, she says. She eats in the staffroom with seven or eight colleagues and they chat about this and that. Once she has eaten her lunch she then gets ready for the afternoon teaching session, by walking across the road to the IT department to collect laptops and takes them to the teaching room. She says she usually does this herself as there is little technical support available. The room belongs to another department and the English tutors just borrow it as they do not have their own teaching space. Although new, large and airy, Sally doesn't think the room is very suitable. For teaching large groups of students, the computer and projectors are poorly positioned and when the students are split into two for smaller seminars, the two tutors have to use large mobile poster boards to divide the room up. Sally says that it took her and her colleague a year of pleading to get these dividing boards. They had wanted more than two boards but the department whose room it is refused, arguing that too many would spoil its 'look'. They also lament the fact that this room is in no sense an English ITE teaching room, in their view, because it does not look or feel like a school classroom at all. This is an issue for their PGCE course, they feel.

As the tutors sort out their teaching materials, we see the students organize the furniture, with tables and chairs grouped and in two halves. They need to find some A3 paper for the session but they struggle to find any – another problem Sally says of not having your own teaching space. The students are relatively young and mostly female, only ten out of thirty-seven are male. Sally sees half of the cohort, her tutor group for 2 days on a weekly basis and has done so since the start of the course. Sally and her colleague, Lynne, go to the side of the room briefly to talk about the Bengali-heritage applicant they think is excellent but who only has a 2.2. We hear them decide that, despite what the VC has said, they will take her. They agree that she has qualities that are more important than a 2.1 honours degree.

In small groups, the students carry out a task that had been emailed to them a few days earlier. A couple of times Sally calls time and organizes the students into a micro-teaching activity, making clear their role when being the teacher and when being pupils. At 2.20 p.m., the student presentations begin, mostly using an old-style whiteboard as there is no access to any IT facilities in the room. The noise from the other side of the room is quite loud and rather distracting for everybody. After each presentation, we see that Sally asks a question of each group and once all the presentations are finished, she gives some general feedback on strengths and areas for development as well as offering a suggestion for a classroom activity – using a washing line to visually display pupils' opinions. After this Sally asks the students to think about what they've learnt today, how they've learnt and what they can take into their own teaching. She hands out a template that they use to complete the task. Finally, Sally draws this part of the session to a close by getting each group to say what they have learned.

At 3.30 p.m. the students move to get into their tutor groups and Sally's students sit around one table. They end up being rather squashed as the table isn't big enough. She then runs the tutorial session, beginning with some school placement-related administrative tasks and ensuring that she collects copies of the students' timetables, important, she says, when sorting out school visits. She then talks to the group about how she will organize school visits using email or even texts to students' mobile phones. She also talks through the documentation needed for these visits and mentions that her visits have a moderating rather than assessment role. She reminds them, it won't be her giving the feedback on their teaching; it will be their mentor. After this she points out that some of her school visit time will be spent talking to each student about general progress, key issues as well as looking at their paperwork. She refers to this as 'establishing a learning dialogue' with them. She then encourages the students to come to her if they experience any problems at all during the placement. Contact via email is the best way she says, but she adds, 'if you're desperate do send a text' and she then gives them all her mobile number again.

Sally talks through the Individual Learning Profiles, how students are meant to use it – through 'negotiation with their mentors' she says and gives a reminder about the paperwork that needs to be completed on a regular basis. Finally, she talks about what to expect in their first school placement, as well as how to use the self-assessment document. She provides each student with a completed example of this document and refers them all to the handbook and the level descriptors. She talks about how to organize the various paperwork in their school files. At 4 p.m. the session finishes; Sally gives out some more admin-related forms and finalizes arrangements for the theatre trip tonight. A student asks Sally to sign a subject audit document, which she does. The students slowly leave and Sally packs away and returns to her office at the end of the day.

Before leaving for home, Sally looks through her diary and sees that she will soon be teaching again on the primary PGCE during their next 'block' on campus. She begins to think about the planning she will need to do and looks at her bookshelves. At around 5 p.m., she skirts around the tent-like structure, locks her office door and leaves to collect her child.

5

Teacher Educators, Proletarianization and the Discipline of Education

In Chapter 2, we reported on studies that explored the ways in which HEI-based teacher educators are conceptualized and argued about in the public sphere, principally through analyses of job recruitment texts (advertisements and job descriptions). We found that the HEI-based teacher educator was produced as a difficult and troublesome category within the exchange relations of contemporary higher education – either as a hybrid form or as an exception to other forms of academic work. In Chapter 3, we looked at the research on the work of school-based teacher educators (often known as mentors), and also at research that investigated the nature of collaborations between school- and HEI-based teacher educators, before moving on to report on the WoTE study and the analysis of data from a small sample of HEI-based teacher educators in England (with some also in Scotland). Through a variety of means, we found that the defining characteristic of the labour of these HEI-based teacher educators was something we called *relationship maintenance*: the communicative activity required to maintain the networks of fragile relationships between schools and HEIs, teachers and student teachers and teacher educators, necessary for partnership teacher education in England. In Chapter 4, we have just presented narratives of experience from four of our sample that were intended to give a rich and concrete sense of the materiality of these teacher educators' work, the details of the specific social situations, the structural constraints and also the historically developed culture and artefacts of ITE in England as well as the possibilities (or otherwise) for these teacher educators' agency.

We now return to the concepts of academic capitalism and, particularly, proletarianization in our attempt to show how the exchange value of teacher educators' labour has declined along with their potential to contribute new ideas and innovations to schools and the wider education system through recognizably academic work. These changes have taken place at the same time that the use-value of what teacher educators have been doing (the defining characteristic we are arguing is *relationship maintenance*) has become more important as partnership ITE in England has become subject more to school-based accountability regimes (such as inspection) and higher education as a whole has also been subject to change. As we discussed in Chapter 3, to refer to academic workers as being subject to proletarianization is not self-indulgent fantasy on our part; Marx and Engels themselves noted that professional groups were subject to the proletarianization process and reduction to 'wage labour' (1888/2008), just as more recent theorists have done (e.g. Debord 1977, Harvey 2010), including those who study higher education (e.g. Guillory 1994).

The proletarianization of teacher educators

In the WoTE project and more recently, we have been working with Marxian concepts we believe are relevant and meaningful in relation to the questions we have asked and the data we generated, situating our examination of the value of teacher educators' labour in the exchange relations of contemporary academic capitalism we described in Chapter 3. This approach to work was taken some time ago in relation to schoolteachers by British sociologists of Education (e.g. Ball 1988, Lawn & Ozga 1988) and we believe it is useful to do so now with reference to teacher educators. We have studied the labour of HEI-based teacher educators as academic work, a topic in which there is some growing research interest. So we have not been calling for a class struggle, pitting proletarianized teacher educators against a putative academic bourgeoisie, seeking pity on their behalf (or, indeed, ours). Nor have we argued that teacher educators alone are vulnerable to processes of proletarianization; in many respects, it is one of the vulnerabilities of academic life under current conditions. Instead, as we outlined earlier, we have been interested in trying to understand the relationships between structure and agency in the work of teacher education, specifically the relationships between culture, socially organized activities and consciousness, and between value, commodities and labour.

Relationship maintenance as necessary work

In Chapter 3, we noted that building, sustaining and repairing the complex and fragile networks of personal relationships that allow initial teacher education programmes, school partnerships and, indeed, HEI Education departments to function were defining characteristics of the work of the teacher educators in our sample. We called it *relationship maintenance*. Whether at the beginnings or ends of days, while driving a car, eating and drinking, at home or in work, we found teacher educators acting both strategically and reactively on the social relations of partnership and institutional life. *Relationship maintenance* is the sort of 'good citizen' work that Acker and Dillabough noted in relation to the women teacher educators in their research, work that incorporates 'social expectations for endlessness that women's work everywhere has at its core' (Acker & Dillabough 2007, p. 301). We believe the narratives of the four women we presented in Chapter 4 illustrate these *expectations* of endlessness in the workplace, as does the work diary data presented in Chapter 3. In Liston's terms, *relationship maintenance* is the 'domestic labour' of HEI Education departments, labour that 'entails the necessary, ongoing and time-intensive (reproductive) tasks of "keeping house" ... recursive and frequently emotional labour' (Liston 1995, p. 104). If Daisy, Anne, Natalie and Sally (like the others in our sample) had not 'kept house' with school partnership coordinators, teacher mentors, professional tutors, fellow lecturers, student teachers – expending emotional energy through nurturing and negotiating relationships at high levels of intensity – then it is more than likely that the programmes they led or worked in would have stalled or even collapsed. Given that Acker, Dillabough and Liston are writing about the Canadian and American contexts, it's also clear that *relationship maintenance*, as we are defining it, is not purely an English (or, indeed, Scottish) contemporary phenomenon but one associated with the cultures of teacher education in HEIs. Cuban (1999), Clifford and Guthrie (1988), Maguire (1993) and others have pointed to tensions between research and teaching in teacher education that arise out of the historical evolution of both teacher education and higher education more generally. We believe this is a tension that has been exacerbated as partnerships with schools (whether formal or informal) have gained in importance in England as elsewhere (cf. Furlong et al. 2009b).

We suggest that there are at least three kinds of pressures that are having the effect of raising *relationship maintenance* to the pre-eminent position it occupied in the work of our sample, specifically with reference to partnerships with schools. First, the requirements of the quality assurance and inspection regimes (Ofsted) and the risks of reputational damage to HEIs who are obliged to compete as 'brands' (and, in England, literally compete for funding on the basis of inspection outcomes) necessitate a relentless focus on being seen to offer 'high quality provision'. 'High quality' is defined in part by the absence of complaints and apparently smooth, bureaucratic arrangements of partnerships with schools. Second, and related, in the wider context of educational reform, HEIs cannot afford to disrupt the social practices of schools 'delivering' those reforms (either in classrooms or in staff rooms), disruptions that may well lead to opportunities for learning by schools and by HEIs but are disruptive nonetheless (Ellis 2010). So, the day-to-day practicalities of the English model of 'partnership' ITE often mean that the teaching methods of schools must be perpetuated in the practices of student teachers even if they run counter to the aims of the HEI teacher education programme. To persist otherwise in an absolute sense would have immediate but also longer term, negative consequences such as the termination of placements or withdrawals from partnerships. *Relationship maintenance* operates both to try to assure this difficult truce in advance and to mop up the mess when practices are (intentionally or accidentally) disrupted. Thirdly, as we have been arguing, we also think it is important to recognize the underlying historical cultures of teacher education as an activity within HEIs and also the residual identities of teacher educators as schoolteachers.

For some in our sample, research was not a motivation to leave school teaching and join an Education department in an HEI. They articulated instead strong commitments to 'spreading good practice', to seeing future generations of school children well taught and also believed they were doing good, 'socially transformative' work (specifically in terms of the class mobility of their student teachers). They produced their own identities as teacher educators in relation to teachers in their partnerships as much or more than they did to their HEI colleagues. We do recognize that the participants in our research had some agency and the capacity to make choices and, as became clear in our participatory data analysis workshop, some of them made choices that were, in a sense, distraction activities. For example, the time spent prolonging an intervention into a school-based problem was, for some, likely to lead to greater feelings of personal success than the same amount of time spent on writing an academic paper or a grant application. That interpretation – suggested by a participant – is not made to blame the teacher educators in our sample but to suggest the strength of the historical cultures of ITE in English HEIs.

The meaning of research in the professional lives of our sample was not only an individual component of their identity work or a potential means of accruing academic capital, however. Some of our participants' contracts did not require them to be research active (the FE college lecturers, including Daisy). And while other institutions did expect research 'outputs', they were reported as making little effort to provide guidance and did not create the conditions (particularly with regard to time) for teacher educators to be successful. In the study of advertisements and job descriptions for HEI-based teacher educator positions we discussed in Chapter 3, we found that 45 per cent of them made no reference to research whatsoever. Professional identities and institutional cultures formed over long periods of time, structured but not determined by academic capitalism and neoliberal technologies of reform and surveillance, can perpetuate an idea of the HEI-based teacher educator as a 'super-teacher', as we suggested previously.

The meaning of proletarianization

As Terry Eagleton (2011) reminds us, '"proletariat" comes to us from the Latin word for "offspring", meaning those who were too poor to serve the state with anything but their wombs' (p. 169). The necessary, nurturing, materially unrecognized and unaccountable *relationship maintenance* work of the teacher educators in our sample allowed organizations such as school partnerships and HEI Education departments to function but simultaneously denied the teacher educators opportunities to accumulate academic capital at a structural level. Founded on a division of labour between the education of teachers and the education of researchers, our data suggests that the work of teacher educators might well support the reproduction of the labour power of research in HEI Education departments from which a class of worker described as 'researchers' alone benefits. Liston (1995) identified this situation in his analysis of teacher education in US universities 20 years ago. These are structural inequalities, with material conditions for teacher educators sometimes profoundly different to colleagues who work on other programmes (in one case, in the WoTE sample, office space shared with six colleagues, for example, rather than one for sole use). For these teacher educators, what is usually part of the academic's workload (teaching, and maintaining the good relationships necessary for teaching) has become intensified to the extent that it is a defining characteristic.

These teacher educators were also required to be intrinsically flexible, adaptable and resilient, capable of dealing with contractual complexity. As regulations and bureaucracy changed, they were expected to respond immediately. As income streams diversified, they were expected to take on additional teaching, with the work associated with Teach First (the UK partner of Teach for America), for example, added to an existing workload of undergraduate- and graduate-level teaching. Moreover, they could even be expected to go beyond their own areas of subject and phase expertise with one of our sample, Sally, a secondary English specialist whose 'day in the life' narrative we presented in the last chapter, required to teach primary science on her institution's Teach First programme. Indeed, in the 3 years since the completion of the WoTE project, Sally had been asked to take on more primary ITE work and was subsequently moved to a 'teaching only' (i.e. non-academic) contract. Soon afterwards, she resigned from the university to take up a post in a school.

This endless flexibility and adaptability was a key characteristic of the proletariat for Marx – a disciplined class of potentially skilled workers but with built-in redundancy (Harvey 2010, p. 318). For the teacher educators in our sample, proletarianization has put them at the sharp end of cuts to budgets as they take on more teaching and *relationship maintenance* on new courses, as they cover for colleagues who had retired or taken voluntary severance and, in one case, as their labour was sold to another university in the same city to run the same course there (Moira, in our sample, organized and taught the PGCE geography courses at the two main universities in her city). The ESRC Demographic Review (Mills et al. 2006) said that a clear career structure didn't exist for teacher educators; in our view, the concept of career (in the conventional sense) was itself problematic for some of our sample.

What proletarianization means, then, for the teacher educators in our sample and, we believe more widely, is that their expertise is unacknowledged and devalued – uncapitalized within the political economy of Education as a discipline – and therefore underexploited in the education of teachers.

The consequences of proletarianization

It is not merely sentimental to comment on the consequences of proletarianization for teacher educators. A lack of a sense of one's future and increasing pressure that restricts one's agency – at the same time as others within HEIs are seen to accumulate the capital required for institutional recognition and advancement – is not a basis for meaningful work, even when aspects of a job are said to be enjoyable. The fact that the proletarianized teacher educator has office space and, sometimes, a car and, occasionally, the flexibility to go to the dentist during the day should not detract from an analysis of their labour within the social relations of academic capitalism. As Horner (2000) points out, we should not confuse:

> … a degree of apparent freedom in concrete labour practices with freedom from the extraction of exchange value from those practices, ignoring the larger social location and organisation of scholarly labour. (p. 5)

We are not claiming that any of the teacher educators in our sample were labouring under a false consciousness but it is not adequate simply to accept that because they said they enjoyed aspects of their work the current situation is satisfactory. The consequences of proletarianization are wider than the individual teacher educator; they are cultural and systemic. Our aim, as we have stated throughout the book, is not to make readers feel sorry for the teacher educator as a category of academic worker, especially at a time of global financial crisis and rising inequality that has led, in England, to significant increases in the use of food banks (http://www.bbc.co.uk/news/business-27032642), for example. Rather, we have been arguing that by doing the work of teacher education differently, teacher educators would be better able to make a difference to schools and the wider education system, including the HEI discipline of Education.

The teacher educators in our sample – like the general population of such academic workers, we suggest – had deep professional knowledge and expertise. We can speculate that this was often the basis on which they were appointed to their posts. It is therefore also reasonable to speculate that people like this could have a much stronger impact on the development of teaching and learning in schools than is currently the case where their labour was mainly directed at sustaining the parallel operation of separate school and HEI activity systems, arbitrating and counselling when smooth operation is disrupted, writing emails, making long phone calls, wiping away tears, and writing this all up as quality assurance. *Relationship maintenance* may be necessary work but it is not necessarily academic work. Indeed, it may be the sort of domestic labour that schools themselves can do or that may not be as necessary if schools take on greater responsibilities for ITE. Indeed, it may not be necessary if the work of learning to be a teacher is itself reconfigured, as we begin to argue in the next chapter. That is not to say that relationships will not sometimes break down but that maintaining them on an even keel will not be quite so important in the overall workload of the HEI-based teacher educator – and certainly not the defining characteristic.

It also seems reasonable to suggest that teacher educators like those in our sample have great potential to engage in research that has genuine impact on professional practice, research in which teachers and student teachers might be genuine collaborators. So our argument concerning the consequences of the proletarianization of teacher educators has two claims: first, school improvement is not being promoted and supported as effectively as it might be; second, the same is true of opportunities for educational research that is motivated by educational interests and that has a real chance of impact on schooling (Ellis 2012b). The consequences are therefore in two directions – for schools and for HEI – but perhaps it is for higher education to take the lead in transforming current conditions, especially given its residual status and national reach.

We take these points up again in Chapter 6 when beginning to articulate our agenda for transformation, but at this point it is worth returning to our earlier discussion of academic capitalism. In 1997, Rhoades and Slaughter, when considering the future development of higher education systems, proposed new forms of 'hybrid' organization and activity in HEIs that might mitigate the effects of the academic capitalism with which they were concerned:

> In our view, if faculty are to regain some influence over their work lives and workplaces, they must move beyond the ideological position of being independent professionals and connect their work and their professional ideology to the interests of the immediate communities and broader publics which they serve. (p. 24)

Theirs is an argument about realigning the motives of academic workers and the objects of academic work to produce knowledge that has value for more than the individual academic capitalist. Burawoy (2011) has made a similar argument in response to the recent crisis of public universities. These are arguments applicable to every academic worker in the discipline of Education and not just teacher educators (cf. Ellis 2012a, Zeichner et al. 2012). Teacher educators are not 'a problem', as our WoTE participants often heard from their institution's research coordinators; the problem is the system. Any progress towards a solution will involve system, by which we mean disciplinary leadership. In our view, Harvey (2010), in his commentary on Marx's *Capital* asks the right question: 'to what degree do our ordinary employments corrupt the courage of our minds?' (p. 187). In answering this question, it is necessary to consider a little more than what we mean by our 'ordinary employments' and, to that end, we now turn to a discussion of Education as a discipline, a particular formation of knowledge and practices that have evolved in higher education settings.

Disciplining education

If Education is regarded as a discipline (sometimes it is not), then teacher education is often regarded as its great weakness. From an institutional-political perspective, Furlong (2013) puts it like this:

> This political weakness has come about largely because, as in the USA (Labaree 2004) as a discipline, education has always been dominated by its involvement with teacher education. (p. 4)

While it is true to say that recent audits of research quality and productivity as the RAE (or REF) have indicated a decline in research in curriculum, pedagogy and teacher education (HEFCE 2009b), it has not always been this way in England so it would be incorrect to attribute, on the basis of causality, any sense of current instability or insufficiency to the association between teacher education and the broader discipline. Prior to the 1980s, with its 'rush to conformity' (Furlong 2005, p. 128), teacher educators, subject to less oversight and fewer constraints, did have some measure of freedom to 'do innovative and creative teacher education work with students' and to become significant curriculum developers (Menter 2011, p. 300). In contrast to criticisms that the work of Education departments was overly theoretical and irrelevant to the practice of the classrooms, teacher educators would often be involved in 'pedagogical or practitioner research' (Murray et al. 2009, p. 946). Given that such work would often be focused upon the craft of teaching, one could argue it was highly relevant to classroom practice if not necessarily theoretically robust or innovative. Nonetheless, there are very strong examples of collaboration between schoolteachers and teacher educators (themselves former teachers) that reached very high levels of academic and professional quality and impact. It is to this part of the history of teacher educators' work within the discipline of Education that we turn next.

The 'disciplines' as ghosts – Spectral agents of higher authorities?

John Furlong's recent book *Education – An Anatomy of the Discipline* (2013) is probably the definitive historical and sociological account of the emergence and evolution of Education as an area of higher education activity in England. It is interesting that, in the introduction to the book, Furlong spends several pages anticipating criticisms of his classification of Education as a discipline at all (pp. 6–13), rather than a 'field', for example, or even a service. We don't intend to offer another account of this emergence and evolution here but will concentrate instead on what we understand by a discipline – in a conceptual and definitional sense – and what working in the discipline of Education might mean for teacher education and the labour of teacher educators. To do so, we build our argument on some of Furlong's earlier work, an edited collection (with Lawn) called *The Disciplines of Education* (2010).

In their introduction to *The Disciplines of Education*, Furlong and Lawn offered something of a generational lament for the passing of an era of established chairs in sociology, psychology, philosophy and history in Education departments, the parallel rise of what they see as the 'practical turn' and the audit culture in higher education. Beginning with a ghostly epigraph from Dickens' *A Christmas Carol*, the impression is of spectral agents of 'disciplinary' authorities frustrated with increasing fragmentation in Education departments and the consequent loss of power and status (in institutional rather than purely personal terms) for those who profess them:

> ... it would seem to us that the earlier post-war foundational model of the patronage of key professors of education and the establishment of key journals has been replaced by a proliferation of professors of education, a disconnection between many of them and older disciplines, with a concentration on useful methods, multiple sources of publication and governmental funding. (Furlong & Lawn 2010, p. 10)

Overall, Furlong and Lawn's argument was interesting at the time for what we saw as the almost complete erasure of Education – the institutional home, the academic and professional practices, the subjects associated with schooling, pedagogy and people. 'Educational research' in Furlong and Lawn's (2010) analysis seemed to us a purely abstract phenomenon; it was not seen as a kind of work – something that *people* do, sometimes. The editors talked of 'disciplines of education' as though a university Education department was entirely made up of a mix of these 'ghosts' from sociology, psychology, philosophy and so on; Education didn't seem to exist in any sense itself as a discipline, outside of these 'older' disciplines' professions *of* it. 'Disciplines', in this argument from 2011, had prepositional advantage, 'disciplinary' perspective bestowing a grammatical distinction. In our reading of this argument, teacher education was merely something that 'disciplines' *have lessons for* rather than as any sort of intellectual field. Moreover, the editors seemed to accept that 'theory' in Education can only come from a 'disciplinary' perspective as the knowledge claims and means of their evaluation can only be determined by these rigorous 'disciplines'. While accepting that the 2011 book was subtitled '*Their Role in the Future of Educational Research*', the editorial position seemed dangerously narrow and undermining. If you profess the sociology or philosophy or psychology *of* an absent or worthless or uninteresting or 'practice'-based phenomenon, you still work in an absent, worthless, uninteresting field where practice has been separated out and relegated to the lower division. It is also, as Biesta points out, a peculiarly Anglo-American construction of the Education discipline that stands in stark contrast to the continental European construction with 'its own forms and traditions of theorising' (Biesta 2011, p. 175) focused on the study of teaching and learning from an *interested* perspective (i.e. one with certain moral, ethical and political commitments).

What was most concerning about the 'disciplines' position was the paradoxical abandonment of Education as a discipline that had its own intellectual energy, interests, action and theory. In part, this position was reflected in current policy then in England and the distaste for undergraduate degrees in Education, the associated promotion of teaching as a 'Master's level profession' and the strange 'M-levelness' of PGCEs where there was sometimes a rush to empirical work in classrooms with narrowly utilitarian aims which were then substantiated as academic inquiry through detailed (not to say repetitive) recitation of 'research methods'.

A key problem with the 'disciplines' position was also that it was inevitably selective in what counted as a 'discipline'. For Furlong and Lawn, sociology, psychology, philosophy, history, economics, comparative and international education and critical human geography were in; linguistics, anthropology, literary and cultural studies, rhetoric and so on were out. Some of these exclusions seemed strange given the history. Chomsky's linguistics (e.g. Chomsky 1965) showed us how children learned by internalizing grammatical regularities through hypothesis testing and had a major impact on how primary and secondary teachers understand child language development and the development of competence in different codes and varieties of language (even as subsequent developments in linguistics have challenged certain Chomskyan assumptions). Michael Halliday showed us the importance of early adult–child interactions for later educational success and prompted us to recognize that educational failure is partly a failure of language (e.g. Halliday 1975). Dell Hymes demonstrated the importance of the anthropological study of language, framed as an ethnography of communication (e.g. Hymes 1973), that was to set the ground for subsequent, seminal studies of classroom interaction by the likes of Courtney Cazden (1988). More recently, Brian Street's early anthropological fieldwork in Iran has led to the development of distinctively 'new' studies of literacy practices and the fundamental distinction between autonomous and ideological models of literacy (e.g. Street 1984). These are strong and useful conceptual contributions to Education from those who worked, at one time or another, on the borders of Education departments or outside them. They are now core ideas at work in Education, not exclusive 'disciplinary' borrowings for which Education should be grateful.

The exclusion of linguistics and anthropology in Furlong and Lawn's account was indicative of a fundamental problem with the 'disciplines' position, which is that if you don't regard Education as a discipline then you have to start making selections from other disciplinary areas to make it up. In making it up, you will inevitably make a selection based on certain criteria that may be neither Educational nor 'discipline' based but narrowly personal. The irony of the 'disciplines' position is also that it runs contrary to contemporary movements – whether interdisciplinary or transdisciplinary – across higher education, where far from being seen as fragmentation and disconnection or the 'proliferation of professors', new modes of enquiry emerge and become institutionalized as they try to ask new questions that are seen as valuable. The field of linguistic anthropology is just one new mode and area of growth, with Shirley Brice Heath (e.g. Heath 1983) one of its notable practitioners. So the 'disciplines' position is not very practical if we are seeking the strengthening of Education as a discipline. It seemed more genuinely a lament for a particular historical moment rather than the end of a tradition stretching back to Aristotle.

The different kinds of conceptual resources available to Education are diverse and powerful and the aspiration to raise the quality of the work that goes on under the heading of Education, whether in teaching or in research, is essential, as we have been arguing. Yet there has to be a sense of a shared endeavour for these aspirations and joint work to have meaning, otherwise the outcome is the intellectual evacuation of Education and a fragmented retreat to the 'disciplines'. Literary and cultural studies scholar Marjorie Garber has written a persuasive and subtle argument about the professionalization of academic work that conceptualizes the relationship between disciplines – in positive terms – as 'envy'.

Discipline envy and the development of productive intellectual energy

In *Academic Instincts* (2001), Garber offered a series of arguments about the future of the academic profession and academic work, especially in the humanities. She surveyed discussions of interdisciplinarity and transdisciplinarity, related histories of the 'professional' and the 'amateur' and the relationship between academics and the public. Garber talks about fields, disciplines and the way they work to distinguish themselves:

> ... a field differentiates itself from, but also desires to become, its nearest neighbour, whether at the edges of the academy (the professional wants to become an amateur and vice versa), among the disciplines (each one covets its neighbour's insights), or within the disciplines (each one attempts to create a new language specific to all its objects, but longs for a universal language understood by all). (Garber 2001, p. ix)

Garber quoted Lewis Carroll's *Alice in Wonderland* to illustrate what she regarded as typical, libidinal disciplinary movements in the academy: 'Everyone wants a seat at the table. But whose table *is* it?' (Garber 2001, p. 59). In her elaboration of 'discipline envy', she distinguished envy from jealousy and aligned her sense of the word with older, more positive connotations (a 'desire to equal another') and with the French *envie* – a 'wish, desire, longing: enthusiasm' (Garber 2001, p. 60). For Garber, discipline envy was normal and inevitable and very old:

> It's the wish, on the part of an academic discipline, to model itself on, or borrow from, or appropriate the terms and vocabulary and authority figures of another discipline. (Garber 2001, p. 62)

Garber used the example of one of her own discipline and institutional homes, Literary Studies, to illustrate discipline envy in action. It is a Literary Studies where Hegel, Kant, Marx, Freud, Lacan, Klein and Derrida are key texts and where the discipline recognizes its obligations to keep apace with broader intellectual movements in society and to use these shared intellectual resources in turn to contribute back to these movements. It is not an argument so much about positioning *within* the discipline but about the relationship of the discipline to other disciplines, to new ideas and social movements and to an increasingly informed public sphere. The outward-looking and intellectually ambitious character of Garber's idea of discipline envy seems a radically different prospect from the essentially inward-looking nature of the 'disciplines' argument. Garber's *envy* poses perceived loss and limit as motive – after Freud, someone else is supposed to possess 'the real thing' in comparison to one's lesser resources – rather than denoting mere introspective jealousy and sorrow. Garber's *discipline* is a set of practices directed towards a shared intellectual goal and distinguishable from doctrine, which, etymologically, has been 'more concerned with abstract theory'. Envy is therefore what keeps disciplines alive, allows for conceptual growth and enables the object of shared intellectual activity to continually transform itself. Discipline envy is intellectual desire directed at the evolution of a set of disciplinary practices. For Garber, it is this space between envy and object, the 'space of disciplinary desire', that we call 'theory':

> And this is why theory always in a sense fails; for when it succeeds, it ceases to be theory and becomes fact or doctrine. (Garber 2001, p. 90)

In our view, discipline envy is a better idea for thinking through the development of a discipline such as Education – and the field of teacher education, in particular – than thinking of the 'disciplines' as ghostly agents of higher authorities with a declining material presence. In the next section, to imagine how discipline envy might stimulate the development of teacher education, we look to the past and the work of James Britton, one of a small group of highly influential teacher educators working at

London University from the 1950s on, as well as other significant projects in the humanities and science education.

Experience, words and mind: James Britton and the intellectual project of teacher education

James Britton worked in teacher education at the Institute of Education from 1954 to 1970 and thereafter at Goldsmith's College. He is well known as the person who introduced English teachers to the work of Lev Vygotsky, following the first translation of *Thought and Language* by the MIT Press in 1962 but his substantive focus was the teaching and learning of English in schools. He is further known for groundbreaking studies in language and learning and the development of writing among school-age children, funded in part by the Schools Council and subject teaching associations. He worked with hundreds of teachers on PGCE courses and the highly distinguished diploma courses possessed by many of the subsequent leaders in the field. He was also a leading member of the Bullock committee that produced the report *A Language for Life* (DES 1975), sometimes regarded as the most significant post-war educational policy document with a wide significance for the whole education system. Indeed, the report remains highly distinctive as a piece of policy with its carefully detailed argument and its references to a wide range of philosophical, psychological, sociological and literary sources.

Britton's project was a pedagogical one and he worked to expand understandings of teaching from 'methods' and 'instruction' just as his contemporary Douglas Barnes enlarged curriculum from 'content'. Britton's teaching saw the student and the teacher – as evolving persons-in-context – engaged in a joint enterprise and he carefully distinguished his own line of thinking from 'child-centredness'. For Britton, it was child-and-adult-centredness and the context was changing as the interaction of learner and more expert evolved.

Taking just one essay by Britton, it is possible to see the depth of intellectual enquiry at work over an extended period of activity. 'Shaping at the point of utterance' (Britton 1980) addresses fundamental problems of teaching (but also rhetorical, psychological and philosophical): spontaneous invention – the relationship between the formulation of ideas and language – the question 'how do we know what we're going to say (or write) before we say it?' – the relationship between speech and writing. 'Shaping ...' is grounded in a seminal empirical study of the development of children's writing between the ages of 11 and 18 (Britton et al. 1975), a study that has had impact internationally inside and outside of Education. In this essay, however,

Britton shows how psychological and psycholinguistic resources from D.W. Harding and Kenneth Lashley; the philosophy of Eugene Gendlin and Michael Polanyi; insights from the North American field of Composition and Rhetoric donated by Janet Emig, Sondra Perl and Mike Rose; the German Romantic poet and dramatist Von Kleist; all are synthesized in Britton's argument that not only must teaching allow space for the exercise of the individual learner's creative agency, but that the production of discourse relies on simultaneous processes of spontaneous shaping and spontaneous interpretation of the world around us. A generation of school teachers and university lecturers in education learned a way of thinking about language from Britton and his colleagues, a way of thinking that has been built on worldwide (e.g. in the US National Writing Project).

Two philosophers in particular were influential on Britton's work, as seen in references to their work almost throughout his writing career, and explicitly in the brief afterword to his *Language and Learning*, first published in 1970: Suzanne Langer and Michael Polanyi. Langer's work encouraged Britton to address the human need to symbolize and therefore question the separation of the cognitive from the affective. Through Langer, Britton was able to offer an account of language as an art that allowed the exploration of 'language and learning' to resist narrowly utilitarian goals. Polanyi, among other things, gave Britton the concepts of subsidiary (of specific words and structures employed) and focal awareness (of meaning, audience, object) to describe the writing process, to emphasize the importance of the guiding and motivating power of focal awareness – and the risks of doing otherwise:

> By concentrating on his fingers…a pianist can paralyse himself; the motions of his fingers no longer bear then on the music performed, they have lost their meaning. (Polanyi 1969, cited in Britton 1980)

The question of Education as a discipline was also of interest to Britton from the preface to the first edition of *Language and Learning* in 1970 through to an essay he wrote for an American collection in the field of Composition and Rhetoric in 1992, two years before he died. Britton's own view was somewhat different to our argument here. He shared the understanding of disciplines, 'properly constituted', as 'dynamic, moveable entities, difficult, even impossible to pin down long enough for the process of definition to get underway' (Britton 1992, p. 47); in other words, as domains of knowledge whose discourses carry power and authority but also offer their practitioners a 'gain in control' (Moffett 1968) and evolve, blend and break away to create productive intellectual energy in a field of practice. Britton also saw the 'disciplines', in the sense used by Furlong and Lawn, as a retreat from Education, and specifically a way out of the complexity of what is going on in schools and classrooms. The hope he expressed was for a 'pre-disciplinary theory' of Education, one that drew on 'psychology, sociology, linguistics but is none of these, a theory that remains close to the observed phenomenon of teaching' (Moffett 1968). Britton wanted to assert Education's concrete closeness to practice as a strength in contrast to the ways in which practitioners of other disciplines presented their work as the pursuit of ever higher altitudes of abstraction.

There is a contradiction in his argument, however, in that the kind of 'consistent, corporate and cumulative activity' (Moffett 1968, p. 49) he associates with disciplinary development is just the sort of activity he argued for in relation to Education and which he himself demonstrated throughout his career. His use of the prefix in '*pre*disciplinary' suggests a forward movement, acknowledging his work as a move forward in the development of the Education discipline and the growth of our knowledge of teaching. When Britton was professionally active in higher education in England, there were great opportunities for the further development of then 'pre-disciplinary' theory, opportunities associated with organizations such as the Schools Council, subject teaching associations such as the London Association for the Teaching of English, publishers like Penguin who produced mass-market paperbacks on Educational topics and a very different cultural identity for the teacher and the profession as a whole. In the years since, it would be something of an understatement to say that we have lost momentum on the kind of project for Education – and for teacher education specifically – that Britton had in mind.

Teachers, research and 'knowledge-brokering' organizations

Around the same time, some of these organizations such as the Schools Council and Nuffield were also funding research and development (often curriculum development) in other subject areas. These organizations seemed to have a role as 'brokers' of knowledge, mediating collaborations between teachers, teacher educators and other stakeholders that were future oriented and focused on innovation. For example, Lawrence Stenhouse's Humanities Curriculum Project funded by the Nuffield Foundation and the Schools Council (Stenhouse 1968) and also the Ford Teaching Project, an initiative that built upon Stenhouse's work, which involved an action research collaboration with 400 teachers in the east of England (Elliott 1976–1977). Initiatives such as these, where teachers and teacher educators collaborated and devised new teaching materials, were notable in becoming 'an established vehicle for curriculum change' (Givens 2000,

p. 71, also see Skilbeck 1990), enabling teacher educators' work to have a powerful pedagogical dimension as well as a publicly disseminated research dimension. However, these forms of research-based, knowledge-producing collaborations between HEI-based teacher educators and teachers often focused on developing new curricula have largely disappeared from the scene in England. There is perhaps only a single notable, current exception to this assertion, namely, the Nuffield Advancing Physics (NAP) project that, at the beginning of the twenty-first century, involved collaboration between various organizations and individuals, including over 300 teachers (Ogborn & Whitehouse 2000, 2001). As Ogborn (2002) noted, the NAP had been only the second, research-based curriculum development initiative he had been involved in over 30 years as a school and university educator. Even when it is claimed that government-instigated curriculum revisions have involved stakeholders (e.g. the review of the science curriculum in 2006), limited attention has actually been given to their views never mind inviting their active participation (Ryder & Banner 2011).

Whereas the Humanities Curriculum Project of the 1970s conceptualized curriculum as grounded in practice, based on systematic inquiry and promoted critical evaluation, the Education Reform Act (1988) and the consequent introduction of the National Curriculum ostensibly removed any structural possibilities for today's teachers and teacher educators to work in the same way. For over two decades now, teacher educators in England have had to function within 'multi-layered accountability mechanisms' (Murray 2007, p. 277), adopt increasingly technical-rationalist approaches in their work (Furlong 1992) and consequently suffer by being marginalized from any research-based curriculum design activities (if, indeed, they have existed) or having much influence on curriculum or pedagogic innovations *per se*. In other words, 'the *pedagogical* dimension of facilitating the development of student teachers' practice is often lost among the variety of roles, functions, and technical acts' (Cuenca 2010, p. 264; our emphasis). The withering away of Education's power as a discipline (political or otherwise) is, we believe, related to the withering away of its core interests in pedagogy. This weakness arises from its disconnection with schools, with teachers, teaching, curriculum subjects and the educational questions that guide research in this area.

Concluding comments

On the basis of the study of recruitment texts and interviews with academic leaders we reported in Chapter 2, it was reasonable to conclude that when universities in England were thinking about what they were 'looking for' when recruiting teacher educators, they wanted an expert 'practitioner' who can 'deliver' research-informed teaching or possibly develop a research 'profile', depending on the institutional context. We thought this position was coherent insofar as it rendered the teacher educator as a difficult or troublesome category, as hybrid or exceptional, and often the subject of some sort of truce with the mission of the university as a whole. The position lacked coherence, however, in that it didn't attempt to reconcile what were often presented as contradictory expectations (high-quality teacher *or* high-quality research) nor was it a position that argued a case for professional education in relation to higher education as a whole. Given that the future direction of higher education in England as elsewhere continues to be uncertain given new policy and funding environments – as well as changing understandings of the aims of higher education as well as patterns of participation – our view was and still is that this question of coherence merits serious consideration. It is also a question, we believe, however differently inflected given the variations in context, that might be asked of teacher education internationally.

On the one hand, we feel that HEIs and the leaders of Education as an academic discipline might well argue for the professional education of teachers as the cutting edge of higher education where knowledge has to meet multiple tests of rigour and relevance in intersecting settings for practice under public scrutiny. Hybridity, from this perspective, is a strength and might be the ultimate goal of all academic work where researchers/practitioners co-produce new knowledge (Gibbons et al. 1994). Teacher educators, under this analysis, do not simply act as a conduit for 'research findings' to teachers, with straightforward implications for practice, but instead their research and teaching collaboratively develops a theory of professional practice that informs and engages with the work of other researchers. So rather than accepting the potentially undermining distinction between 'basic' and 'applied' research, the academic work of the teacher educator potentially explodes such a polarity with a focus on practice-developing research that also develops a theory of practice (cf. Chaiklin 1993). The hybrid vigour of the teacher educator therefore arises from their capacity to work with teachers and other stakeholders to develop new knowledge across multiple social settings and at different levels of specialization and abstraction. This meaningful interpretation of hybridity is one that Zeichner has started to pursue in the US context (Zeichner et al. 2012).

If, on the other hand, proximity to practice and 'professional credibility' and 'relevance' are over-riding factors, there are at least two important questions to answer: first, given that ITE in England, for example, is mainly school based, do both partners (schools and HEIs) need the same forms of expertise? It seems reasonable to assume that, appropriately resourced, school teachers would win the credibility argument every time and ITE would therefore need to be located in schools – an unusual situation indeed if one looks around the world. Expecting HEI-based teacher educators to act as 'super teachers', as external facilitators of reflection, as quality assurance consultants or as 'enthusiastic' and 'resilient' examiners of assignments is surely an unsustainable model of higher education's involvement in teacher education. Traditionally, at least, suitability for academic work has not relied on personal qualities alone. Second, when the teaching profession – in the way Evetts (2009) understands a profession as a knowledge-creating collective, built on principles of collegiality and trust – is being transformed through political reform, in England and internationally, what does 'professional credibility' and, more vitally, professional knowledge actually mean? When governments seek to specify the professional knowledge base (for however laudable, 'socially just' ends), then the highest levels of professional credibility can only ever be achieved by civil servants and politicians. The involvement of higher education only slows down reform, from a politician's perspective; so professional credibility can only accrue to those who align themselves with the politics of the day. The choice here seems to be one of defending the current arrangements or going along with the reformist agenda that is focused on increasing the importance of the 'super teacher' teacher educator and 'experience' in schools and the increased marginalization or even exclusion of higher education.

These positions might seem extreme – acceptance of a reduced professionalism and often inferior arrangements for teacher education that are always an immediate subject to the dominant influences of neoliberal reform agendas; defence of the *status quo* and a resistance to change or the articulation of a new vision for the professional education of teachers in collaboration with HEIs – but they do capture something of the nature of the challenge. In this book, we are arguing for the third position, one of transformation, and that will begin with a better articulation of the arguments in the public sphere. Our view is that teacher education as an academic field within the discipline of Education in HEIs in England and elsewhere needs to build these arguments more effectively, to make a case more persuasively and to do so with the same rhetorical power as those who argue from the reformist position. In the next and final chapter of this book, we begin to provide some of the premises and propositions that can support such an argument about the transformation of teacher education through reconfiguring the academic work and in relation to an expanded notion of the professional work of teaching.

6

Public Universities and the Profession of Teaching: Towards an Agenda for Transformation

In this book, we have been examining the work of preparing school teachers from a cultural-historical perspective and with a particular focus on the labour of HEI-based teacher educators. We have focused on the English context in some detail but have also drawn on international comparisons and analysis. In discussing our own researches, we have situated them within this international arena and have argued that what we found in England is consonant with situations in other countries around the world. While we may have used Marxian concepts such as proletarianization in our own studies, other researchers in the United States, Canada and Australia have used feminist or labour theories to show how the work of teacher educators in HEI settings falls disproportionately on groups (often women without doctorates) who struggle to achieve recognition and advancement within the value systems and exchange relations of higher education.

We have argued that England presents an interesting case of what can happen to teacher education (as a set of practices within a higher education discipline as well as professionally) when it becomes subject to the reform agendas of a residual, 'statist' state that also has commitments to markets, financialization and the techniques of New Public Management. We have also suggested that the underlying questions and issues are not unique to England. They can be identified internationally in countries where some globally 'travelling ideas' (Seddon et al. 2013) about educational reform have touched down. Equally, other possibilities and other systemic arrangements can be identified – in countries such as Finland, for example, countries that are often the focus of policy tourism rather than serious analysis. In short, as we argued in Chapter 5, if we want to get the discipline of Education right, we need to get teacher education right. And, as we argued in Chapter 1, if we want to ensure the best possible preparation for new teachers and also ensure their retention and their continued professional development, HEIs have an important contribution to make and we need to get that right too.

The relationship between higher education and the professions more broadly merits further consideration. Most HEIs have long histories of professional education of one form or another as well as providing a pool of graduates for further preparation. Internationally, HEIs also have a gate-keeping role in many professions and sometimes quasi-regulatory functions (in England, for example, by officially recommending Qualified Teacher Status – effectively the license to teach – and judging cases of professional suitability). So any agenda for transforming teacher education as academic work must also consider the nature of teaching as a profession and how higher education relates to professionals and professional organizations as well as their clients and the wider society. While granting absolute autonomy to higher education and professional groups at any cost and in all circumstances is undemocratic, simply using higher education to open and close the gates of professions on terms prescribed by the state is equally undemocratic, as we shall argue. Of course transforming teacher education as a field of higher education cannot be for the good of teacher educators alone. Using higher education as a delivery mechanism for political agendas driven by electoral cycles is, however, also an unsustainable position.

In this chapter, we develop our agenda for the transformation of teacher education, for reconfiguring the academic work in order to prepare teachers better. It is an agenda that grows out of the English context but seeks to address some wider structural problems and to learn from analyses of international experience. We take a different approach to Furlong (2013) while sharing much of his analysis. In his elaboration of a new future for Education as a discipline (Furlong 2013, pp. 183–199), Furlong separates out professional education, knowledge mobilization and research. Instead, we argue that these activities must be integrated: the discipline of Education should re-focus on core educational questions and interests, help to re-invigorate the professional work of teaching as a collaborative community and, in order to achieve these goals, review how the higher education discipline faces the profession and the wider publics. To suggest some ways in which this integration of activities might be enabled for wider systemic benefit, we focus on knowledge and knowledge creation. We do so not because we believe that it is research *per se* that will solve the problems we have identified but because different conditions for producing and accessing professional knowledge are needed, different to those in the current situation. We seek conditions that are likely to be more conducive to the development of the profession *and* the discipline. To begin our discussion of the possibilities for transformation, we turn first to higher education and the role of 'public universities'.

Public universities – Democratizing institutions with relative autonomy

A democratic constitution, not supported by democratic institutions in detail, but confined to the central government, not only is not political freedom, but often creates a spirit precisely the reverse, carrying down to the lowest grade in society the desire and ambition of political domination.

JOHN STUART MILL (1871, cited in Gutmann 1999, pp. 283–284)

Amy Gutmann (1999) has argued that public institutions such as schools and universities are essential to the effective functioning of open, participatory and democratic societies and in doing so she follows in a strong philosophical tradition (e.g. Dewey 1927, Popper 1945, Tocqueville 1848). The key contribution these institutions make to this functioning is the creation of conditions and the provision of public space for deliberative discourse. Schools and universities provide (or at least might provide) preparation for participation in deliberative processes and universities have responsibilities to contribute to this deliberation at an advanced level in the public sphere through their commitment to the creation of new knowledge through research and the mobilization of that knowledge for the greater good of society. As Gutmann argues, the extent to which a society may be described as democratic is 'the extent [to which] citizens and their accountable representatives offer one another morally defensible reasons for mutually binding laws in an ongoing process of mutual justification' (Gutmann 1999, p. xii). As Furlong (2014) has put it, it is this 'commitment to the "contestability of knowledge" that marks universities out as unique in society' (p. 8). The consequences of the failure of public institutions noted by John Stuart Mill in the quotation above are that top-down control by the state creates in populations the expectations of being continually guided by that state to the detriment of their human agency and creativity.

As Furlong also points out, HEIs are complex institutions, a 'conglomeration of earlier concepts and organisational forms' (2013, p. 168). Nonetheless, historically, it is possible to identify the 'public university' as a type of HEI that has evolved both to widen participation in post-secondary education at the same time that new kinds of publics have, at least in part, been created through their responsibilities for public deliberation. These public functions of HEIs have included what Dewey (1927) referred to as the development of a 'collective intelligence' in society but also the creation of the open social structures that permit the deliberative public discourse and (inevitably partial) flows of knowledge necessary for our democratic existence. Public universities contribute both the new knowledge and the public space and channels of communication for the mobilization of that knowledge so as to enable new developments and allow new ideas to take hold. They do so in sometimes unpredictable and fragile ways – ways that Karl Popper (1945) described as 'piecemeal social engineering' – but without being subject to an over-determining and controlling ideology, no matter how utopian (or even totalitarian) in intent. Public universities can therefore be institutions of democratic education in the fullest sense and the majority of HEIs in English-speaking countries were long regarded as such – at least in ideal-type terms – for example, the four-year colleges and research-intensive state universities in the United States and the civic and modern universities of England. Indeed, as Holmwood (2011) points out, until fairly recently, the ideal of the democratic and democratizing university as a public institution was explicit in higher education policy in England: the Robbins Report of 1963 saw universities as 'serving democratic citizenship by improving debate and the capacities of citizens' (Holmwood 2011, p. 7) and the Dearing Report of 1997 (commissioned by the Conservative Education Secretary Gillian Shephard) argued that the benefits of higher education went beyond the individual's accumulation of social and cultural capital but that HEIs were necessary in order to:

> sustain a culture which demands disciplined thinking, encourages curiosity, challenges existing ideas and generates new ones; [and to] be part of the conscience of a democratic society, founded on respect for the rights of the individual and the responsibilities of the individual to society as a whole. (Dearing Report 1997; para. 5; cited in Holmwood 2011, p. 9)

At the core of the sustenance of this culture is the academic freedom of those who work in universities and colleges and the relative autonomy of HEIs from political control. We say 'relative autonomy' as arguments for absolute autonomy within a participatory democracy are difficult to justify, especially when the creation of new knowledge and the critique of existing intellectual traditions are at stake. As Gutmann suggests, though, good arguments for relative autonomy can be made, especially for professional schools in HEIs (the example she gives is law): if professional schools are intended to produce competent professional practitioners but also critical scholars of the professional practice then 'one might conclude that the standard of relative autonomy justifies state licensure but not control of the content of legal education' (p. 174). In order to prepare critical scholars of the professional practice, the principle of academic freedom for the HEI professional school educators is essential. Such freedom allows them to 'assess existing theories, established institutions, and widely held beliefs, according to the canons of truth adopted by their academic disciplines…provided that they remain within the bounds of scholarly standards of inquiry' (p. 175). Gutmann stresses the constraints within which this freedom operates: 'the bounds of scholarly standards of inquiry' set a higher threshold for academic freedom than general freedoms for citizens. Academic freedom is conditional on maintaining these standards within the mutual bonds of an academic community; it is not the right of an academic to do as she or he pleases. Academic expertise is exercised within a framework of scholarly as well as public responsibilities.

The challenge to this view of the public university and of necessary academic freedom – of higher education having a democratic *and* democratizing function *per se* – has significantly grown in strength in recent years. Wendy Brown (2011) characterized the change as a shift from understanding higher education as 'a social and public good to […] personal investment in individual futures, futures construed mainly in terms of earning capacity' (p. 23). From this perspective, HEIs have become disengaged from society, have had their roles as public institutions eroded by the state and replaced by the right of government always to represent public interests everywhere. In this analysis, the student becomes a consumer whose choices are guided by market rationality and the university becomes a brand that jostles for position in global rankings such as the Shanghai Jia Tong. There need be no relation to society in the way we have been describing here. This decline of the public functions of the university coincides with the decline of other democratizing institutions. According to Brown:

> Neoliberal rationality recognises and interpellates the subject only as a speck of human capital, making incoherent the idea of an engaged citizen, an educated public or an education for public life. (p. 23)

Critiques of these challenges to the ideal of the public university have been very strong in the humanities in recent years, as Furlong (2013) notes. Many scholars (e.g. Collini 2011, Holmwood 2011, Lye & Vernon 2011) have been active in their reassertion of the democratizing function of the public university against the forces of neoliberalism. In some respects, they are part of a long tradition of advocates of the liberal arts and, like their predecessors, they argue that the current crisis is not simply a result of recession and budget deficit – not an inevitable 'product of necessity', as Lye and Vernon put it (2011, p. 5) – but as a contemporary manifestation of historical contingencies that can be changed. Perhaps less discussed is the role of academics themselves in bringing about the current situation as they have competed for grants and titles, counted citations and fellowships and generally strived to create the spectacle of the star researcher within the exchange relations of academic capitalism. We should remember that some have thrived within the current system while others have struggled to survive. Nonetheless, change is possible and the work of sociologist Michael Burawoy offers us one, we think, important and relevant example of a future orientation.

Four types of knowledge and the public university

In his proposal for reimagining the public university, Burawoy (2011) places a knowledge problem at its centre. Public universities, says Burawoy, have been dealing with dual governmental pressures: the *commodification* of knowledge and the *regulation* of knowledge production: 'If commodification raises the question of knowledge for whom, regulation raises the question of knowledge for what?' (p. 31). In reframing the problem, as Ellis (2013a) describes, Burawoy delineates two broad categories of knowledge – instrumental and reflexive – under which four types of knowledge are included: *professional* knowledge and knowledge for *policy* purposes (the 'instrumental' category); and *critical* knowledge and *public* knowledge (the 'reflexive' category). Burawoy contends that the public university must attend to all four types of knowledge even while the balance between the four may vary. Instrumental types of knowledge are those that allow certain kinds of work to get done; reflexive types of knowledge require dialogue about values and purposes underlying the necessary instrumentalities and also about the wider aims for society. Burawoy claims that it is reflexive types of knowledge that are at greater risk given current emphases on the instrumental but also accepts the importance of instrumental types of knowledge. He also specifies two dimensions of participation as 'audience' in his typology under the heading of *autonomy* and *heteronomy*. Autonomy signals the academic channels of communication that are essential to sustain scholarly productivity and the creation of new knowledge; heteronomy signals the essential relationships with the policy sphere as an aspect of a liberal democracy as well as relationships with the wider publics and responsibilities to citizens in society as a whole. The relative autonomy of public universities to create and contest knowledge is granted in relation to certain responsibilities towards democratic politics and society in general.

Ellis (2013a) has adapted Burawoy's typology with specific reference to teacher education and it is reproduced in Table 6.1.

Table 6.1 Knowledge in and for teacher education in the public university (after Burawoy)

	Autonomy (Academic audience)	Heteronomy (Extra-academic audience)
Instrumental knowledge	*Professional* Knowledge arising out of research designed to develop educational practice such as teaching	*Policy* Knowledge associated with the application of research designed to improve educational practice in achieving political goals and democratically accountable aims for society
Reflexive knowledge	*Critical* Knowledge arising out of the critical evaluation of research and traditions of research that seek to develop educational practice; knowledge that situates this research in wider intellectual and historical contexts	*Public* Knowledge carried through deliberative discourse about the development of educational practice in the public sphere, knowledge that stimulates the wider give-and-take of reasoned justification in society

Source: Adapted from Ellis (2013a, p. 210).

The relationships between these types of knowledge are complex and not easily managed. For these reasons (and others) Burawoy's typology does not lead to 'scaleable' policy 'solutions' on a 'management by objectives' model that have been so popular in countries such as England. So, for example, just as the creation of professional knowledge cannot be 'short-circuited' in the service of policy, critical knowledge must be communicated with the wider publics; otherwise there are risks both to the development of public knowledge, society's understanding in general and the development of the critical knowledge that is the 'collective conscience' of the university (pp. 32–33). Burawoy asserts that:

> …the public university gives weight to each of the four types of knowledge, requires them to be in dialogue with each other and recognises their interdependence *even as they are in an antagonistic relation*. Each knowledge depends on the other three. (p. 33; our emphasis)

The uneasy, integrative balance Burawoy is proposing is not permanent but must be continually re-made. As Ellis (2013a) points out, to use Burawoy's definition, the professional knowledge of teacher education arises out of a range of activities that might take place in a school setting. It is instrumental in its orientation towards the improvement of education – but is nonetheless deliberative, systematic and subject to social (professional, scholarly) processes of justification. If this form of professional knowledge does not seek to have a relationship with policy, it will, as Burawoy puts it, 'wither away'. Equally, if teacher education does not seek to inform policy then it removes itself from society. If the realm of policy tries to co-opt professional knowledge for its own political ends, though, or if policy seeks to buy professional knowledge through narrowing research priorities, then both professional and policy knowledge are devalued. These instrumental types of knowledge also require the reflexivity provided by critical examination both within the academic community and outside of it. Instrumental forms of knowledge associated with the development of an educational practice such as teaching must be situated within the historical, intellectual contexts in which such activities have evolved as well as in deliberations over the direction of society and its moral and ethical interests. The balance is one of sustaining relative autonomy in order to achieve wider benefits beyond the academy – into schools, the profession and the wider society.

Ken Zeichner (e.g. Zeichner et al. 2012) has been explicitly arguing for a similar shift in the practices of teacher education in the United States. Recognizing the actual and potential distinctive strengths of university coursework in pre-service programmes – the development of adaptive expertise among student teachers developed in their engagement with research-based knowledge – he nonetheless makes a broader argument for reconfiguring the practices of teacher education:

> ...the preparation of teachers for democratic societies should be based on an epistemology that is itself democratic and includes a respect for and interaction among practitioner, academic and community-based knowledge. (p. 5)

So, like Burawoy, for Zeichner this reconfiguration is also, in part, a knowledge problem where the professional knowledge of HEI-based teacher educators has traditionally been conceptualized in 'non-egalitarian' ways with school teacher (delivering 'findings' to 'end-users', for example) but it is also a problem of the relationship between higher education and society. In arguing for a more democratic teacher education, Zeichner and colleagues used the concept of 'hybrid spaces' – designed social environments that bring actors from different fields of practice together to work on a potentially shared object (Engeström et al. 1999). Within such spaces, they argued, new knowledge and practices might emerge from the dialogic sharing of expertise by various partners (professional, policy and community, for example). Distributed knowledge of the different types we have been discussing in this section can inform the development of teacher education as a higher education activity and as a professional activity.

Strengthening these public functions of HEIs as a whole and, within that, attempting to negotiate the difficult balance between professional, policy, critical and public knowledge in teacher education are also likely to have benefits for the profession of teaching. It is to professions and professional work that we turn next, again emphasizing the requirement for relative autonomy (on a collective rather than an individual basis) and the need to reject the extremes of what Gutmann (after Walzer 1981) calls the 'insolence of office' and the 'ossification of office' (pp. 77–78).

Professions – Distributed agency and collective creativity

Division of labour, complementarity of expertise, and collaboration between different professional groups – and the development towards multiprofessionality – are essential parts of distributed agency.

MIETTINEN *(2013, p. 131)*

Reijo Miettinen's (2013) analysis of institutional change and learning in the Finnish comprehensive school system identifies distributed agency and boundary-expanding collaborations as drivers of innovation and success. Distributed agency as a concept is particularly useful to Miettinen as it allows him to explain at a macro-level how the twin approach to economic innovation and the development of human capabilities in Finland has been achieved. Finland has prospered, according to Miettinen, because of its 'enabling' welfare state, a state without controlling 'statist' aspirations, that has recognized the economic context of human activities without resorting to economist or human capital 'solutions'. Agency – the capacity and the freedom for human beings to act with responsibility – has been widely distributed within Finnish society, along with trust in agents that has in turn led to confidence in their capacity to innovate. He quotes the head teacher of a Finnish school to illustrate what distributed agency has meant for the Finnish teaching profession:

A great deal of confidence is placed in teachers [in Finland]. A great deal of power, responsibility and freedom is given to them, and they deserve it. No ponderous control mechanisms are needed. In many countries inspections and constant testing form a barrier to creativity and misdirect the teachers' energy. (Miettinen 2013, p. 133)

Rather than presenting an argument for the re-installation of older forms of individual (and, one might argue, undemocratic) professional autonomy, Miettinen draws on an evolutionary theory of innovation and creativity to argue for the relative autonomy of professional groups such as teachers. Centralized control (albeit from an elected political class) enacted through standards 'inhibits the emergence of variation, which constitutes a constitutive foundation for development' (p. 139). Strong national policy levers lead fields in 'predetermined directions'; they do not stimulate the 'emergence of new associations, experiments, sets of tools, and complementary expertise within the field' (Miettinen 2013). In terms of teachers and teaching, such mechanisms lead to the 'ossification of office' (Gutmann 1999) – the withering away of agency, the capacity to take responsibility, confidence and the growing reliance on guidance or specification from the centre. 'Ponderous mechanisms of control' produce, in the end, what John Stuart Mill called the desire and ambition of political domination from within professions and societies as a whole. The lesson from Finland's success, argues Miettinen, as well as lessons from successful cultures of innovation elsewhere, is that variations in perspective, knowledge and resources, subject to open deliberation within communities in which diverse and often difficult collaborations are encouraged, are much more likely to lead to real-world problems being addressed and innovative new ideas and ways of working being developed. In terms of schools and teaching, this involves distributing agency to the profession as a collaborative community (among many such communities).

In proposing 'collaborative community' as a theoretical model of contemporary professional work, sociologist Paul Adler rejected two earlier ideal types of professional community, *Gemeinschaft* (collective but rather like craft guilds) and *Gesellschaft* (an example being experts for hire). Adler believes that neither of these historical types of community is adequate for current and future conditions as they both have limited capacity to support the creation and mobilization of new knowledge. So what he refers to as the 'functional pressures' of marketized forms of organization and more bureaucratic, hierarchical forms 'are encouraging the emergence of the collaborative form' of community as a new phenomenon (Adler et al. 2008, p. 364). A vital focus of these functional pressures is the capacity of professional groups to respond to problems of practice with new ideas and, in making his analysis, Adler is careful not to sentimentalize community as a form of collective organization, as can happen. Indeed, it is the knowledge-creating affordances and potential for innovation of the three different

Table 6.2 The strengths and weaknesses of three different organizing principles of professional work for knowledge creation identified by Adler et al. (2008)

Organizing principle	Strength	Weakness
Community (as traditionally understood)	High levels of trust facilitate access to tacit knowledge held in shared practices and promote local knowledge creation	There is a risk of insularity within communities as 'silos' and the closure of outward-looking innovation
Market	Flexibility and responsiveness to new problems of practice are encouraged	Knowledge creation tends towards short-term 'solutions', a 'race to the bottom' and limited significance
Hierarchy	Managerial techniques of control can effectively disseminate already codified knowledge	Bureaucratic hierarchies provide weak incentives to create new knowledge and lack sensitivity to tacit knowledge

Source: Adapted from Ellis (2013b).

organizing principles (market, hierarchy and community) of professional work that are absolutely fundamental to Adler et al.'s general argument. Table 6.2, adapted from Ellis (2013b), summarizes the different strengths and weaknesses of these organizing principles for professional knowledge creation (Adler et al. 2008).

Adler et al. claim that their new, theoretical model of *collaborative community* integrates the three organizing principles. Collaborative community as a model addresses hierarchical forms of management, market pressures and competition while simultaneously transforming traditional community principles. It does this by encouraging responsiveness to new work situations and the exercise of distributed agency and by challenging local knowledge creation to have much wider, public impact. It recognizes economic contexts without regarding the economics as over-determining; similarly it accepts that organizations (such as schools) often have strong vertical accountabilities but proposes that horizontal and rhizomatic collaborations are more likely to lead to innovative new ways of working for the greater good.

Building on Adler's research and neo-Vygotskian theory, Ellis (2013b) has argued for collective creativity as a key criterion of professional work and *professional creativity* as a defining characteristic of the professionality of teaching. Centrally relevant to this idea of professional creativity is the Vygotskian concept of intellectual interdependence, the 'process of construction of new ideas through the transformation of old ones in a communicative process' (Valsiner & van der Veer 2000, p. 12). It is the contribution of these new and transformed ideas to the knowledge base of a collaborative community that allows the profession to grow and develop, exercise its collective, distributed agency and act with responsibility and trust. The development of professional creativity then becomes a core focus of any programme of teacher preparation – through an induction to the profession's systems of ideas and their modes of interrogation, the professional teacher is able to respond to unpredictable situations with new ideas and practices on an independent basis but drawing on a shared, collaboratively built knowledge base and, potentially, contributing something of significance to it.

The more open view of professions we have been discussing in this section – and the implicit shift away from understanding professionalism merely as a question of the individual professional's rights and authority – has focused particularly on the responsibilities for knowledge creation based on values and ideals that are subject to deliberation within a collaborative community that looks outward, not only towards clients but to the wider society. As such, we are arguing that a profession such as teaching can have productive relationships on the one side with other professionals such as teacher educators and other academics in the public universities and, on the other, with the parents and communities of the children they teach and, beyond, to society. Understood in this way, understood as 'the degree of autonomy – or insulation from external control – necessary to fulfil the democratic functions of office', professionalism, as Gutmann (1999) has put it, '*completes* rather than competes with democracy' (p. 77; our emphasis). Professions – like public universities – are not barriers to the improvement of public services such as teaching; they are not part of 'The Blob' as one former English Education Secretary (and one former US Secretary for Education) put it (see Chapter 1). Their claims to relative autonomy derive from their demonstrable expertise in specific domains of human activity and their responsibilities to sustain and develop the historically accumulated knowledge held within those domains. Together, professions and public universities might contribute more fully to the necessarily dialogic process of improving education, schools and, specifically in relation to our interests in this book, the preparation of teachers. In the next section, we look at how such relationships between public universities and a public sector profession such as teaching might be conceptualized.

Public universities and the profession together: Transforming teacher education

The types of – and the qualities of – relationships between public universities and the teaching profession are key to our arguments in working towards an agenda for the transformation of teacher education. In many respects, these aspirational relationships – specifically those that are formed around the initial preparation and continuing development of teachers – might be described as 'coconfiguration', a concept that has emerged within the CHAT tradition of organizational learning research (Engeström 2007b). Coconfiguration has been defined by Engeström as 'an emerging, historically new type of work' that relies on responsiveness to context; 'continuous relationships of mutual exchange' between stakeholders; continual evaluation and development of key processes; the active involvement of stakeholder groups that might usually be defined as 'end-users'; the creation of boundary zones or 'third-spaces' where collaborators move beyond their own practice settings and mutual learning on the part of all collaborating partners (2007b, p. 24). Engeström relates coconfiguration to the CHAT concept of 'knot-working' (joint activity that is focused on complex, boundary-spanning problems that emerge, expand and require multiple forms of distributed expertise to address).

Knot-working as a description suggests that 'no single actor has the sole, fixed authority' in the collaborative creation of new knowledge (Engeström 2007b); it differs in kind from older forms of partnership and collaboration in its focus on 'negotiation, exchange and trading' and its characteristic features of being *transformative* in radically expanding (growing, making more complex) the potentially shared objects of activity; of emphasizing *experiencing* in its attention to personal, embodied engagement with material artefacts in working on the future of an activity; of being *horizontal* as a form of dialogic learning that ties knots between different activity systems and actors and unfolding in *subterranean* ways – sometimes 'underneath the radar' and barely noticeable as it sets the ground for new kinds of knowledge and practice to emerge and making them viable (p. 38). In other words, coconfiguration is an attempt to conceptualize collaborative partnerships between multiple organizations that have different priorities and primary objects but that come together to work on particularly 'knotty', socially complex and challenging problems. This form of collaborative working requires designed social spaces for the partners to come together and trust each other and the shared commitment to do things differently, to produce some new ways of working that will lead to the creation of new knowledge that can be capitalized for the public good. Coconfiguration as a concept therefore recognizes the political economy of professional learning as well as the high levels of trust and personal engagement that are required.

Understanding the relationships between public universities and the teaching profession as being based on the coconfiguration of new knowledge-laden practices is a different prospect to understanding them as forms of 'partnership', as we have come to describe them most often in England. Even the scarce and hard to identify kinds of 'collaborative partnerships' between schools and HEIs that Furlong and colleagues categorized (Furlong et al. 2000) are based on more traditional hierarchical relationships between partners, more vertical lines of 'accountable' collaboration and more stabilized and stabilizing models of 'knowledge transfer'. Knowledge that might have been produced within what was often regarded as the gold standard of the 'research-informed' collaborative teacher education partnership was nonetheless deemed 'applied' and highly situated, requiring the higher education partner to 'abstract' it in order to have wider meaning. From this perspective, it is always higher education that 'adds value' to what schools do; there is little or no acknowledgement that there might be a strong (or even stronger) reverse contribution.

Instead, knowledge produced through coconfiguration explodes such a distinction between 'basic' and 'applied' modes of knowledge creation; it is knowledge that has to be tested within multiple and intersecting communities of practice, that has to meet the standard of trustworthiness and reliability set by different systems of justification. Good arguments can be made that knowledge created through such 'hybrid' practices of coconfiguration are stronger and more likely to lead to innovation and positive change in complex, changing and societally significant practices such as school teaching. The kind of hybrid practices of coconfiguration that might potentially characterize a transformed teacher education aligns very closely with the mode of knowledge production identified by Gibbons et al. (1994) as Mode 2. Although Gibbons et al.'s research arises out of the sociology of science rather than CHAT, their work is relevant to our argument as it emphasizes the complex social mediations necessary for the emergence of new ideas.

Hybrid practices of coconfiguration and Mode 2 knowledge production

Gibbons and his colleagues argued that traditional (Mode 1) knowledge-producing communities (experimental science being their key example) have responded in complex ways to demographic and technological change as well as economic globalization. The scale of this response has been significant to the extent that a new mode of knowledge production is identifiable, Mode 2.

Mode 1 knowledge production is determined by academic interests that are 'primarily cognitive' in orientation (Gibbons et al. 1994, p. 1). Organizationally, this type of knowledge is produced and accessed within communities that tend to be hierarchical and 'homogeneous' and prize autonomy. By contrast, Mode 2 knowledge production is characteristically heterogeneous, transdisciplinary, socially accountability and reflexive. Mode 2 knowledge arises out of hybrid social practices that are at the same time academic and non-academic, instrumental and critical, personal and political. Mode 2 offers a good description of a highly networked, participatory, diverse and distributed mode of knowledge production, one that relies on distributed agency and trust between its partners.

However, as Nowotny et al. (2003) later reflected, the Mode 2 idea was taken up differently across disciplines, also noting that these different and sometimes ill-informed appropriations of the idea came from those with 'most to gain...struggling to wiggle out from under the condescension of more established...disciplines' (p. 179). Also, as Nowotny et al. noted, many appropriations of Mode 2 erased the political economy of the concept with the knowledge created not being contextualized within the value systems and exchange relations of the institutions within which they are put to use. In terms of higher education research, for example, some appropriations of the Mode 2 idea might ignore the realities of academic capitalism as the dominant system of values and exchange, as we discussed earlier. Nonetheless, Mode 2 does at least offer a useful metaphor for the shift in the ways that knowledge is produced across the professional, policy, critical and public domains. It also differs from older arguments within Education about 'practitioner' knowledge that is 'insider' knowledge and in opposition to 'outsider' or more publicly available knowledge.

Indeed, at the core of Mode 2 is a fundamental cultural–historical idea: a 'dialogical process, an intense (and perhaps endless) "conversation" between research actors and research subjects' (p. 187). This blurring of identifications of investigators, end-users, 'scientific peers' also contributes to the blurring of categorizations of basic and applied research that is implied by coconfiguration as well as confounding traditional linear chronologies of 'projects' (with the absolute finality of dissemination and subsequent impact). As such, Mode 2 offers a challenge to conventional understandings of research and knowledge production, especially in higher education settings, as much as it is a description.

The nature of this challenge is indicated by the use of *agora* to represent the hybrid spaces of the original Mode 2 theorization (Gibbons et al. 1994). *Agora* suggests marketplace as well as meeting point and therefore seeks to account for different kinds of capital while underlining the political economy of the knowledge-creating situation. Gibbons originally used hybrid space to describe the 'meeting point of a range of diverse actors, frequently in public controversies' (p. 167). Hybrid space related to the third Mode 2 principle of 'organizational diversity'. In Nowotny et al.'s (2003) reflections, however, *agora* is a more explicitly political and economic zone of proximal development – it is literally a social market that is a space for the growth of new ideas:

> The *agora* is the problem-generating and problem-solving environment in which the contextualisation of knowledge production takes place. It is populated not only by arrays of competing 'experts', and the organisations and institutions through which knowledge is generated and traded, but also by variously jostling 'publics'. It is not simply a political or commercial arena in which research priorities are identified and funded, nor an arena in which research findings are disseminated, traded and used. The *agora* is a domain of primary knowledge production – through which people enter the research process, and where 'Mode 2' knowledge is embodied in people and projects. (p. 192)

From the field of organizational science, Paul R. Carlile also emphasizes the personal, political and economic implications of creating new knowledge at the boundaries of different organizations that come together in such Mode 2 knowledge-creating, collaborative communities:

> For all groups involved, it is their ability to create and explore the 'knowledge potential' at the gap, where these practical and political abilities go hand in hand in transforming knowledge and generating innovation at a boundary. Recognising the political and practical issues that arise is consistent. (Carlile 2004, p. 29)

The potential relationships between public universities and the teaching profession, embodied in the joint work of departments or faculties of Education and schools, and enacted in the labour of HEI-based teacher educators and teachers, can be conceptualized as one such difficult and antagonistic *agora*. In structural terms, at least, the channels of communication and the possibilities for collaboration exist and, in England, have been mandated for 20 years, even though their potential as complex zones of proximal development has not been realized systemically.

Zeichner et al. (2012) have used the concept of 'horizontal expertise' from CHAT to speculate on the possibilities for more egalitarian and democratizing teacher education practices, where partners' 'different interests, values and practices' can be socially mediated and a new and potentially transformative shared object might emerge (p. 7). Zeichner has also drawn on Engeström's (2007b) concept of knot-working to suggest that the participation of multiple actors with diverse expertise needs to be more fluid and object (or problem)-oriented than conventional institutional structures allow in order to improve public education. Again, such an injunction to approach teacher education as knot-working and the related call to shift our understandings of research and knowledge creation to align with a Mode 2 perspective, present a serious challenge to business-as-usual in the academy, as well as in the schools. For many HEI-based research-active teacher educators, it would mean a different kind of knowledge is prioritized and valued – knowledge from the *agora* rather than knowledge from the *acropolis*. In other words, knowledge that has use-value in practice situations, that has been produced within rule-governed systems of scholarly inquiry but that also connects to the policy sphere in critical ways and that is deliberated in the public sphere – this becomes the knowledge that is valued, the knowledge that makes a difference in terms of the improvement of practice in relation to articulated aims for education and that might also contribute to the growth and flourishing of the academic discipline of Education. This challenge and the required shift mean there is something to give up for all potential collaborators in shared aspirations for a collective gain. Understood from this perspective – and understanding hybridity etymologically – hybrid practices of knowledge production within relationships of coconfiguration are likely to be more generative, more socially accountable, reflexive and supportive of the better preparation of teachers, the agency and creativity of the profession and the strengthening of the Education discipline and the possibilities for meaningful work of those who labour within it.

Distilling some principles: Public universities and the profession working together on transforming teacher education

Following on from the earlier discussion, we now offer five principles that might guide the wider society, HEIs, schools and communities in changing the terms of the debate about the preparation of teachers and transforming teacher education:

Principle 1: *Higher Education Institutions are public institutions – public universities – with democratic functions that merit relative autonomy and require academic freedom to be sustained in order to complete their work in society and, specifically, make a qualitative difference to the preparation of teachers for schools.*

Principle 2: *The discipline of Education in public universities can model the difficult, integrative balance between professional, policy, critical and* *reflexive knowledge required of all disciplines and should seek new associations and new relationships inside and outside of the academy in order to realize this balance.*

Principle 3: *The profession of teaching is a collaborative community deserving of the distributed agency afforded by an enabling state and with responsibilities for the development of the collective, professional creativity that makes a positive difference to the education of young people in schools.*

Principle 4: *The relationships between higher education and the profession around the preparation of teachers might be understood as coconfiguration of new forms of activity rather than merely structural partnerships and channels of communication that seek to reproduce existing practices.*

Principle 5: *Coconfiguration of teacher education activity can produce strong, Mode 2 forms of research and development that has systemic impact as well as having benefits for all collaborators, including HEI-based teacher educators.*

Reconfiguring the academic work

The aspirational principles we have presented are necessarily wider than higher education alone or the profession alone. In elaborating them, we have sought to integrate HEIs as public institutions with the wider society in terms of their knowledge-creating functions at the same time as conceptualizing the profession of teaching as a collaborative community with obligations to exercise responsibility (specifically in relation to professional knowledge) with relative autonomy and a commitment to democratic rather than narrowly political accountability. In both cases, we have emphasized the importance of trust (within society and within and between institutions) and distributed agency – the responsibility to act with freedom of movement within a specific domain of knowledge and practice with a future orientation. Our principles arise out of research in human learning and development, cultural–historical psychology, organizational theory and the sociology of science and of the professions. They are also underpinned by an evolutionary theory of innovation in which greater variation in the social situation of development creates the conditions for the emergence of new ideas, new tools and new associations (Miettinen 2013).

In this final section of the chapter and of the book, we turn to specific actions that lead out from these principles and that might contribute to our agenda for transformation of teacher education. In doing so, we move away from the broad landscape of professional education and the proposals for coconfiguration we have been outlining and turn specifically to higher education and the possibilities for reconfiguring work within academic contexts. As with the book as a whole, the actions we propose speak specifically to the English context, our context as authors, which, as we have argued, is one that presents an interesting case internationally. As Seddon et al. (2013) point out, however, within the context of globalization, there are certain 'travelling' education reform ideas that ' "touch down" within national territories and systems of education' and are intended to disturb 'the spatial, temporal, relational and knowledge boundaries that once secured specific national forms of teacher professionalism' (p. 4). We believe that teacher education has become a key focus for these globally travelling education reform ideas with their narrow focus on 'teacher quality' (measured in terms of student test scores). So while the localizations of these ideas can vary from setting to setting, we believe that our general argument – along with these principles and the following actions – has a relevance that is wider than England.

Action 1: Create the conditions for change through powerful arguments in the public sphere

Towards the end of John Furlong's *Education – An Anatomy of a Discipline* (2013), he comments on the 'massive undermining' he sees of the post-war situation of higher education and teacher education, specifically, in England. He asks how university Education departments have responded:

> They have been silent. Very few people will stand up and say, 'In the face of the current challenges, this is why education must be a university-based discipline; this is what the university can contribute that is distinctive, that is important.' (Furlong 2013, p. 167)

To create the conditions necessary for transformation on the basis of the principles we have just set out, it is essential that educationalists (whether they are HEI-based academic workers or school-based professionals, trade unionists or others) contribute to arguments about education, schooling, teachers and teaching in the public sphere. This necessary action is rhetorical – making strategic interventions in the ongoing public debates that have been dominated by speakers from neoconservative or neoliberal, and very often, narrowly party-political positions driven by electoral cycles. The failure of educationalists both to initiate debates and to change the terms of public debates has been startling, with very few exceptions. Likewise, the failure of senior leadership in HEIs over more than 20 years to define and protect the academic freedom of their Education departments has contributed very strongly to our current situation. On the one hand, institutional anxiety (whether over securing income from sometimes high-volume ITE programmes or over general issues of political compliance) has cumulatively eroded the independence and critical agency of HEI Education departments to the extent that, in England, the final say in quality assurance has been handed over to the government inspectorate. At what point did the leaders of our public universities agree that control over the content of the teacher education curriculum would be determined by politicians and compliance with it would be policed by civil servants with automatic right of access to university premises and access also to institutional policies, people and data? That point of principle is lost; it will be difficult but not impossible to argue it back. Rather than defensively arguing back to the reformers on their terms, it will be necessary to argue in the wider public sphere (as the reformers have learned to do so well) with new propositions about the importance of academic freedom and distributed agency for the real improvement of public services such as schools as well as for the general health of society.

On the other hand, educationalists in public universities also need to assert the importance of engagement with schools and the importance of teaching as an area of critical inquiry and research activity that leads to the creation of useful knowledge with both exchange value and impact. Strong arguments can be made for research that arises from coconfigurations of teacher education activity that challenge the short-termist and economist criteria of judgements made under conditions of academic capitalism. In England, the 'impact agenda' (under which researchers are required to demonstrate the difference their research has made to culture and practice (under the rubric for the 2014 Research Excellence Framework (REF 2011))) can support such arguments for a more engaged and powerful educational research. Mode 2 knowledge production is valued in many disciplines and rewarded appropriately within institutional and scholarly communities as well as in promotion and career development structures. Again, instigating the change in criteria will be difficult, especially when in some contexts educational researchers have been advised to model their activities mainly on those in 'basic' disciplines such as sociology or psychology. But again, change is possible and it will be through motivated, strategic and skilful rhetorical action in the public sphere that transformation in the conditions for the preparation of teachers can begin to be realized. This action sets a challenge for senior leaders in HEI Education departments who we believe have primary responsibilities for creating the conditions for change.

Action 2: Design professional learning around complex understandings of practice

The fragmentation of ITE programmes has frequently been identified as a barrier to their success in preparing teachers (cf. Grossman et al. 2009; Smagorinsky et al. 2003). Taking classes in HEIs (in the United States, sometimes even in different departments or faculties) and then undertaking some supervised teaching in neighbouring schools, it is said, has contributed to a theory–practice divide that limits the full and rich appropriation of research-informed ideas in the practical work of teaching. Efforts to address this problem have led to HEIs holding lectures on school premises as well as initiatives such as teacher residencies (e.g. Zeichner and Sandoval 2013) or internships (e.g. Benton 1990), where the majority of the time on the ITE programme is spent in the workplace, in schools and teaching in classrooms. Support and feedback have provided a mentor and there is a contribution from an HEI that 'wraps around' the work-based learning of the student teacher and is more limited in scope than many traditional ITE programmes, particularly those in the United States (although it is worth noting that residencies and internships vary considerably).

While attention to space and time is important when planning designs for learning, the way in which practice is conceptualized is also vital in programmes of professional preparation such as ITE. The learning of a professional practice carries with it the sense of being involved in the critical dialogue within and outside the profession about aims and purposes in relation to wider discussions about the future of society, to which the practice might contribute. Professional learning also necessarily involves engagement with the historically accumulated and evolving knowledge base of the profession so that knowledge and practice are seen as different emphases on the same activity: knowledge in practice becomes the focus of development in a professional learning programme and the challenge is to reject the persistent Cartesian dualism that still underpins many approaches to formal education.

Magdalene Lampert's (2009) essay 'Learning Teaching in, from and for Practice: What do we mean?' raised many important questions about how practice might be conceptualized when we design teacher education programmes. In concluding that paper, Lampert posed what she thought was the 'most important question' about 'use of the word practice in relation to learning teaching': whether it should be understood as an individual phenomenon or whether it is 'something created and maintained by a collective and learned by participation in that collective' (Lampert 2009, p. 32). In this book, we have been arguing that practice is a collective phenomenon, whether a collective of teachers, of teacher educators or a hybrid and internally differentiated, 'knot-working' collective that comes together to work on a tricky but societally important problem such as preparing school teachers. By understanding practice as a collective phenomenon, 'stretched over' (to use Lave's term [1988]) individuals within a community that shares historically accumulated knowledge and with a future orientation to those practices that are subject to public deliberation, we are more likely to improve teacher education.

Although it is now sometimes fashionable to dismiss communities of practice theories as 'mere' participation and 'learning by doing' in idealized, always collegial groups, we believe it is worth re-visiting one of the key tenets of the original idea from Jean Lave and Etienne Wenger's research on situated learning (1991). The essential dynamic at the heart of any genuine community of practice is the 'continuity–displacement contradiction'. The continuity–displacement contradiction is Lave and Wenger's central challenge to a reproductive or acquisition view of learning based on a static notion of knowledge to be internalized and a stable set of practices to be routinized (ironically, a view of professional learning that has characterized many reformist positions on ITE down the years that regard it merely as training in 'what works'). Innovation is impossible within such a closed system of acquisition and reproduction. Instead, the continuity–displacement contradiction at the core of a community of practice puts the personal engagement and embodied perspectives of newcomers and old-timers into productive tension and one far from sentimentalized understandings of 'community':

> Newcomers are caught in a dilemma. On the one hand, they need to engage in the existing practice, which has developed over time: to understand it, to participate in it, and to become full members of the community in which it exists. On the other hand, they have a stake in its development as they begin to establish their own identity in its future. (Lave & Wenger 1991, p. 33)

Lave and Wenger's argument is that this contradiction involves conflict and tension (between the expert or more experienced and novices) centred on learning, participating and a developing sense of identity. It is through the 'continuity-displacement contradiction', arising out of the negotiation of increasing participation for 'newcomers with their own viewpoints', that the conditions are established for the generation of new knowledge:

> ... legitimate peripheral participation is far more than just a process of learning on the part of the newcomers. It is a reciprocal relation between persons and practice. This means that the move of learners toward full participation in a community of practice does not take place in a static context. The practice itself is in motion. (p. 3)

Understanding practice as being 'in motion' is important when designing professional learning programmes for a number of reasons in Lave and Wenger's theory but for our argument in this book it helps us to bridge the theory/practice divide we discussed earlier in this section as well as extend the concept of distributed agency. In analysing his research on practice development in commercial and industrial settings, Engeström (2007b) discusses the frequently noted 'gap' between good ideas and 'implementation' in traditional forms of intervention. In proposing coconfiguration as a more generative description, he notes that when it has seemed to work well 'the personal and the collective, as well as the immediate and the future oriented, seem to merge' (p. 36). Echoing Lave and Wenger, Engeström notes the importance of a 'projective identity' (Gee 2003) for the participating practitioners and personal engagement in human learning and development. The research and evidence we have been drawing on throughout the book suggests to us that the more complex understanding of practice we have been advocating is also more likely to improve the retention of teachers within the profession.

A related concept from communities of practice theories that we believe is useful in our argument in this section is that of 'core blindness', the sedimentation of practices in the work of 'old-timers' or experts and the invisibility of the purposes and rationale driving them and the accessibility of the knowledge with which they are in a dialectical relationship. Lave and Wenger associate this phenomenon with 'full' participation by those at the core of a practice, those that might have a desire to sustain the *status quo*. One of the positive outcomes of the tension produced by the continuity–displacement contradiction is the potential opening-out of discussion about purposes and rationales between experts and novices and the associated increased visibility and insight on the part of experts and experienced practitioners. One of the ways in which this new insight is achieved is through participation in other, related practices and by comparing the experiences of participating in both so that the premises and possibilities of both are illuminated.

Recent work on 'pedagogies of enactment' in ITE (e.g. Grossman et al. 2009) has started to unpack how a practice-based teacher education curriculum might work. The focus in this research on identifying 'core practices' of teaching stresses the importance of attending 'to both the conceptual and practical aspects associated with any given practice' (Grossman et al. 2009, p. 8). This line of research and development also shows how such 'core practices' might be 'decomposed' or 'parsed' so as to develop something like a functional grammar of teaching. Critics of this approach might argue that the decomposition of practices into separate elements on the basis of effect size (however determined) is reductive insofar as it isolates the technical aspects of an action without attention to its sociocultural, historical, political and economic contexts (i.e. its meaning) as a human activity. Another criticism might be that, with such an emphasis on teachable routines, learning and instruction are designed in response to data-driven representations of a whole class of children rather than responsiveness to the real, actual children, perceived in the interaction. Nonetheless, researchers in this recent tradition have made great efforts to embody the outcomes of their inquiries in the content of their institutions' teacher education programmes. New possibilities for what might go on in HEI-based teacher education classes have been demonstrated, where a sharp focus on specific routine or 'moves' is modelled and demonstrated by the HEI-based teacher educator, inviting the student teacher to appropriate such 'approximations of practice' (Grossman et al. 2009, p. 8) by way of a form of cognitive apprenticeship.

Our view is that the development of a pedagogy of enactment is worthwhile when it draws in the school-based teacher educator, mentor or cooperating teacher. 'Decomposing' a real episode of teaching in the course of that teaching – utilizing strategies for collaborative teaching, modelling ways of working and then creating opportunities for student teachers to join in while they become increasingly independent – is likely to be a very powerful means of scaffolding school-based, practice-focused ITE. But it will not necessarily produce the continuity–displacement contradiction that will allow the practice to develop nor will it necessarily enable the personal engagement in critical dialogue about the aims and purposes of the practice under examination, the sort of engagement that is likely to build the agency of the beginning practitioner and encourage them (as a key attribute of this design for professional learning) to develop the intellectual interdependence necessary for professional creativity. We do not dismiss 'core practices' as an approach to teacher preparation but ask whether, within the kind of reconfigured academic work we are seeking, a pedagogy of enactment in ITE is the sole or main responsibility of the HEI-based teacher educator. It seems to us that working with teachers to keep a practice 'in motion', stimulating continuity–displacement contradictions (within schools but also within HEI departments and faculties of Education) and maintaining a close focus on the knowledge-in-the-practice, enabling both access to it and the development of it, is a more appropriate and beneficial role for the HEI-based teacher educator.

Action 3: Rebuild the research programme in teaching and teacher education around theory-building, cross-setting intervention research

Stimulating continuity–displacement contradictions, as we have suggested earlier, is also something that might contribute to the development of the HEI-based teacher educator as an academic worker as well as the discipline of Education. These developments might be attained not only by creating opportunities to keep the school-based practices of teaching in motion but by allowing the challenges surfaced by such processes to develop new lines of inquiry in higher education's educational research communities. As Ellis has argued (2011b), stimulating the professional creativity of teachers is also likely to lead to the stimulation of teacher educators' professional creativity, in the terms described, one manifestation of which might be the growth and the strengthening of robust research programmes in teaching and teacher education. The Education panel in the 2008 UK RAE noted that these once strong areas of research activity in higher education (see also Chapter 5) had withered away somewhat while other areas such as the sociology of education and experimental studies had strengthened (HEFCE 2009b).

The cultural–historical perspective that has informed this book regards closeness to practice and engagement with theory as twin aspects of the same processes of research and development. Rejecting dualistic understandings of mind and behaviour, cultural–historical theory (and its interventionist iteration, CHAT) requires us to attend to the materiality of human activity in order to understand the development of higher psychological functions. So in teacher education activity, the division of labour (between schools and universities but also *within* universities) matters for the kinds of new knowledge that it is possible to create and mobilize within activities that are designated as 'research'. CHAT, specifically, offers us the tools of an interventionist tradition with a developmental purpose and works from an interested standpoint. So the approach to research and development we have been advocating – drawing particularly on Gibbons' and Nowotny's concept of Mode 2 knowledge production and Engeström's coconfiguration – necessarily challenges the 'disinterested' standpoint that is often still advanced as a key criterion of academic research. A researcher following the approach we have been outlining does not seek to tell school teachers what to do, for example, by delivering 'findings' to 'end-users'. As Engeström noted in his reflections on design experiments, such a linear view of knowledge *transfer* 'ignores what sociologists teach us about interventions as contested terrains that are full of resistance, reinterpretation, and surprise' (2007b, p. 369). Rather, researchers in this new and emerging tradition seek the development of *'critical design agency* among all the parties: researchers, teachers, and students or, respectively, researchers, managers, workers, and clients' (p. 370; emphasis in the original). As Ellis (2013b) has suggested:

> In terms of the current relationships between university education faculty and school teachers, this aspiration for the collaborative exercise of different agencies presents a formidable challenge, not the least of which is a risk associated with the general approach which Engeström describes as 'paternalistic manipulation' (p. 382). But the challenge also extends to school teachers who must also be willing to give up their rugged or 'heroic' individualism and the tacit wisdom of the 'craft' in order to gain greater control over their own activities and their development through an active engagement in the production of new knowledge. (Ellis 2013b, p. 213)

The possibilities for rebuilding the research programme in teaching and teacher education are not limited to CHAT-informed approaches, of course. For example, recent developments in design-based intervention research in the United States give a strong sense of the nature and scale of the change that is required, as Gutiérrez and Penuel (2014) have suggested when arguing that the education research community needs to understand the limits of generalizability:

> This requires a shift in focus of research and development efforts, away from innovations designed to be implemented with fidelity in a single context and towards cross-setting interventions that leverage diversity (rather than viewing it as a deficit). It also suggests the need to focus some research and development projects on the design of new organisational routines and infrastructures for improvement.... (Gutiérrez and Penuel 2014, p. 22)

Such an approach to research and development might support the strengthening of the discipline of Education overall at the same time that it builds the research programme in teaching and teacher education. In some ways, it runs contrary to the advice given to some Education departments in England in the recent past which has been to model their intellectual activities on the 'foundational' disciplines such as sociology, philosophy and psychology. Focusing research on 'the design of new organisational routines and infrastructures for improvement' is a rather different prospect but it is also one that is found in many higher education disciplines (such as engineering, for example) and for which there is probably greater evidence of flourishing in countries such as the United States. This approach is also one that would support the integrative balance between professional, policy, critical and reflexive types of knowledge that we discussed earlier.

With particular reference to policy, we also believe that a rebuilding of the research programme in teaching and teacher education along these lines would be more likely to connect to the policy audience and help to inform debates in more constructive ways than has sometimes been the case. In a recent article in *Educational Researcher*, Christine Sleeter questioned the impact of much teacher education research on policy making (Sleeter 2014). In making her analysis, Sleeter referred to studies by Nelson et al. (2009) and the American Educational Research Association's Panel on Research and Teacher Education (2005) that reported on the research–policy interface. Nelson et al. interviewed 65 US policy makers and found a distrust of much educational research, including 'experimental studies, viewing them as too narrow' (p. 147). Instead, Sleeter observed, 'they paid most attention to evidence of interventions that can be applied systemwide, are locally relevant, and are sustainable' (Sleeter 2014). Building a research agenda around cross-setting interventions that show how good ideas 'interface with local realities' (Sleeter 2014) while also generating theory (with CHAT being one good example of how this might be achieved) is also a way in which HEI-based teacher educators – with the wealth of knowledge and experience they usually bring from professional settings, combined with academic and research training – might contribute more productively to the education of teachers. At the same time, this work will be of the type that will (and in fact, already does elsewhere in HEIs) enable the flourishing of the discipline as well as the individual teacher educator.

In setting out five principles and three actions that, together, might offer in outline an agenda for the transformation of teacher education, we are aware that much more goes on in Education departments and faculties than the initial or 'pre-service' education of teachers. As a discipline, Education is not only concerned with schools nor only with teachers nor, indeed, young people just in their role as students or 'pupils'. But we want to recognize that there is a historical problem, one that has come to fore with some intensity recently in England and elsewhere, which means that in order to get Education right in higher education and, indeed, in order to get teaching as a profession right, we need to do something about the work of HEI-based teacher educators. The issue, as we have shown, is wider than universities and schools, however, and this final chapter has been our attempt to lay out an agenda for positive change based on key principles and urgent actions that take into account the place of higher education and the profession of teaching in society generally as well as the more immediate and local concerns of one occupational group, no matter how important their work.

A different future is possible

We began the book with a speech by a fictional principal of a College of Education, Prin, as she celebrated the graduation of the final year students – as it turned out, the final ever to graduate from that college. It was a situation that William Taylor had cruelly caricatured in *Society and the Education of Teachers* in 1969, a situation in which:

> a diluted form of gracious living was engaged in by a largely spinster staff, in an impressive if educationally unsustainable and draughty building at the end of a mile long drive, ten miles from the nearest town. (Taylor 1969, p. 205)

As Maguire and Weiner (1994) noted, women teachers who became teacher educators were vulnerable to a form of proletarianization from the earliest beginnings of the training colleges, working long hours, having salary reduced for board and lodging, teaching a 'main subject' and a 'subsid' and being required to 'involve themselves in the social and religious life of the college' (p. 125). In several respects, it could be inferred, they would have been better off if they had stayed in schools. Maguire and Weiner also pointed out that these women's work in training colleges was a form of emotional as well as social and intellectual labour. What we have referred to as *relationship maintenance* in our own research – a defining feature of contemporary HEI-based teacher educators' work in England, we argued – was built in to the identity of the training college educator from the start:

> Their role was educational as well as related to the emotional well-being of the students. Even those in higher positions had a part to play in the ethos of 'caring' and commitment to the students' psychological health. (Maguire and Weiner, p. 126)

Maguire and Weiner noted the dedication to the job and the sense of 'mission' that these women teacher educators felt, often to their own personal economic and career detriment. Over time, men took the senior posts and the higher salaries in these colleges, even though they may have been less qualified as the women they managed. Women did what was necessary to keep house and ensure that the job of educating teachers was carried out with as little disruption as possible.

In this book, we have argued that the division of labour between academic workers in higher education departments and faculties of Education continues to reproduce a system in which a specific group – the teacher educators – find it hard to extract reward from their labour within a predominantly academic capitalist system of values and exchange. The problems of this current system are wider than the individual teacher educator's career development; they reflect both a weakness within the wider higher education discipline of Education and the reduced form of professionalism that has become available for teachers. Paying attention to what teacher educators do and how they work with student teachers matters because it reveals both the vision and direction of travel for Education as a discipline as well as the forms of agency that are available for the profession. So our argument in this book has been partly a call for the re-imagining of HEIs as public institutions and partly a call for the re-imagining the professionalization of teaching.

In making our argument, we have been careful not to defend the *status quo* and to try to justify that what goes on presently in the name of teacher education is always perfect. Instead, we have tried to suggest a way of reframing the debates about educating teachers on the basis of principles concerned with the relationship between higher education and society, HEIs and the professions and the challenges of societal development in a globalized world where economic innovation and the development of human capabilities (rather than human capital) are not mutually exclusive (Miettinen 2013). Our principles and our proposed actions are supported by the research evidence: for example, creating challenging tensions with teachers' communities of practice in order to improve outcomes for students has a good effect size, according to syntheses of the 'best evidence' (Timperley et al. 2007); evaluations of teacher education policy across Europe have long identified the need for new kinds of active systemic relations between HEIs and schools that go beyond the structural connections of partnership (Buchberger et al. 2000). But we have not written a book that argues back to reformers on their terms; we have not sifted the evidence for variation in effect size in experimental studies that seek to raise test scores. We have not sought to defend teacher education against the reformers. We have sought to develop a research-informed agenda for transformation and to that extent we have followed Lakoff's advice: 'Do not use their language. Their language picks out a frame – and it won't be the frame you want' (Lakoff 2004, p. 3).

Our proposed actions are, perhaps, the part of our agenda that is most specific to England. As we have said, we do believe that England presents an unusual case internationally in terms of the relationship between public services and market principles, neoconservatism and neoliberalism and a residual welfare state that has controlling rather than enabling instincts. Nevertheless, the three actions we have outlined might have a relevance beyond the English context. They do, at least, emphasize the fact that while there are no quick fixes, the way we prepare teachers probably does need to change.

Discussions of the future of teacher education are often imbued with a deep fatalism, sometimes (but not always) supported by sociological critiques of a totalizing and deterministic kind. We end by repeating an obvious but sometimes hidden assertion: another future is possible. The ruptures and resistances that complicate educational reforms can be brought together in systematic ways to provide a reasonable and reasoned alternative to the dominant perspectives; 'non-reformist reforms', as Lipman (2011) described them, collaborations among diverse groups that can set new parameters for possible solutions, transforming not reforming or defending teacher education as it is.

Bibliography

Abell, S. K., Dillon, D., Hopkins, C.J., McInerney, W.D. & O'Brien, D.G. (1995), "Somebody to count on": Mentoring/intern relationships in a beginning teacher internship programme. *Teaching and Teacher Education* 11, 2: 173–188.

Acker, S. (1997), Becoming a teacher educator: Voices of women academics in Canadian faculties of education. *Teaching and Teacher Education* 13, 1: 54–72.

Acker, S. & Dillabough, J.-A. (2007), Women 'learning to labour' in the 'male emporium': Exploring work in teacher education. *Gender and Education* 19, 3: 297–316.

Adler, P.S., Kwon, S.-W., Heckscher, C. (2008), Professional work: The emergence of collaborative community. *Organization Science* 19, 2: 359–376.

Adonis, A. (2012), *Education, Education, Education: Reforming England's Schools*. London: Biteback Publishing.

Alexander, R.J. (1984), Innovation and continuity in the initial teacher education curriculum. In Alexander, R.J. (Ed.) *Change in Teacher Education: Content and Provision since Robbins*. London: Holt, Reinhart and Winston.

Apple, Michael W. (2001), Markets, standards, teaching and teacher education. *Journal of Teacher Education* 52: 182–196.

Ball, S.J. (1988), Staff relations during the teachers' industrial action: Context, conflict and proletarianisation. *British Journal of Sociology of Education* 9, 3: 289–306.

Ball, S. (2012), *Global Education Inc. New Policy Networks and the Neo-liberal Imaginary*. London: Routledge.

Bazerman, C. (2004), Speech acts, genres and activity systems: How texts organise activity and people. In Bazerman C. & Prior P. (Eds) *What Writing Does and How It Does It: An Introduction to Analyzing Texts and Textual Practices*. Mahwah, NJ: Lawrence Erlbaum Associates.

Beloff, M. (1968), *The Plateglass Universities*. London: Secker & Warburg.

Benton, P. (Ed.) (1990), *The Oxford Internship Scheme*. London: Calouste Gulbenkian Foundation.

Berliner, D. (2014), Effects of inequality and poverty vs. teachers and schooling on America's youth. *Teachers College Record* 116, 1. Retrieved from www.tcrecord.org on 1 April 2013. ID Number 16859.

Berry, A. (2007), *Tensions in Teaching about Teaching: Developing Practice as a Teacher Educator*. Dordrecht: Springer.

Biesta, G. (2011), Disciplines and theory in the study of education: A comparative analysis of the Anglo-American and continental construction of the field. *Pedagogy, Culture and Society* 19, 2: 175–192.

Blake, D., Hanley, V., Jennings, M. & Lloyd, M. (1997), The role of the higher education tutors in school-based initial teacher education in England and wales. *Teachers and Teaching: Theory and Practice* 3, 2: 189–204.

Bok, D. (2013), *Higher Education in the US*. Princeton, NJ: Princeton University Press.

British Educational Research Association/Royal Society of Arts Inquiry into Research and Teacher Education (BERA 2014), The role of research in teacher education: Reviewing the evidence, Interim Report.

Britton, J. (1980), Shaping at the point of utterance. In Freedman, A. & Pringle, I. (Eds) *Reinventing the Rhetorical Tradition* (pp. 61–66), Conway, AR: L&S Books for CCTE.

———. (1992), Preface. In Herrington, A. & Moran, C. (Eds) *Writing, Teaching, and Learning in the Disciplines*. New York, NY: Modern Language Association.

Britton, J., Burgess, T., Martin, N., McLeod, A. & Rosen, H. (1975), *The Development of Writing Abilities 11–18. (Schools Council Research Studies)*. London: Macmillan Education.

Britzman, D. 1991/2003), *Practice Makes Practice: A Critical Study of Learning to Teach*. Revised edition. Albany, NY: State University of New York Press.

Brown, W. (2011), The end of educated democracy. *Representations* 116, 1: 19–41.

Bruner, J. (1986), *Actual Minds, Possible Worlds*. Cambridge, MA: Harvard University Press.

Buchberger, F., Campos, B.P., Kallós, D. & Stephenson, J. (Eds) (2000), Green Paper on Teacher Education in Europe. Umea: Thematic Network on Teacher Education in Europe, Umea University.

Bullough, R.V. & Draper, R.J. (2004), Making sense of a failed triad: Mentors, university supervisors, and positioning theory. *Journal of Teacher Education* 55, 5: 407–420.

Burawoy, M. (2011), Redefining the public university: Global and national contexts. In Holmwood, J. (Ed.) *A Manifesto for the Public University* (pp. 27–41). London & New York, NY: Bloomsbury Academic.

Byrne, E.M. (1978), *Women and Education*. London: Tavistock Publications.

Calhoun, C. (1994), Explanation in historical sociology: Narrative, general theory, and historically specific theory. *American Journal of Sociology* 104, 3: 846–871.

Cameron, D. Speech to the CBI Monday 19 November 2012, available online: http://www.number10.gov.uk/news/speech-to-cbi/ (last accessed 24 May 2013).

Carlile, P.R. (2004), Transferring, translating, and transforming: An integrative framework for managing knowledge across boundaries. *Organization Science* 15, 5: 555–568.

Carrillo, C. & Baguley, M. (2011), From school teacher to university lecturer: Illuminating the journey from the classroom to the university for two arts educators. *Teaching and Teacher Education* 27, 1: 62–72.

Cartaut, S. & Bertone, S. (2009), Co-analysis of work in the triadic supervision of preservice teachers based on neo-Vygotskian activity theory: Case study from a French university institute of teacher education. *Teaching and Teacher Education* 25: 1086–1094.

Carver, C. & Feiman-Nemser, S. (2009), Using policy to improve teacher induction critical elements and missing pieces. *Educational Policy* 23, 2: 295–328.

Castells, M., & Himanen, P. (2002), The Finnish model of the information society. Oxford, England: Oxford University Press.

Cazden, C.B. (1988), *Classroom Discourse: The Language of Teaching and Learning*. Portsmouth, NH, Heinemann.

Chaiklin, S. (1993), Understanding the social scientific practice of 'understanding practice'. In Chaiklin, S. & Lave, J. (Eds) *Understanding Practice: Perspectives on Activity and Context*. Cambridge: Cambridge University Press.

Chomsky, N. (1965), *Aspects of the Theory of Syntax*. Cambridge, MA: MIT Press.

Christie, D. (2003), Competences, benchmarks and standards in teaching. In Bryce T. & Humes W.M. (Eds) *Scottish Education: Post-Devolution*. Second edition. Edinburgh: Edinburgh University Press, 952–963.

Clifford, G.J. & Guthrie, J.W. (1988), *Ed School: A Brief for Professional Education*. Chicago, IL: University of Chicago Press.

Cochran-Smith, M. (2008), The new teacher education in the United States: Directions forward. *Teachers and Teaching: Theory and Practice* 14, 4): 271–282.

———. (2009), The new teacher education in the United States: Directions forward. In Furlong, J., Cochran-Smith, M. & Brennan M. (Eds) *Policy and Politics in Teacher Education: International Perspectives*. London: Routledge.

Cole, M. (1996), *Cultural Psychology. A Once and Future Discipline*. Cambridge, MA: Harvard University Press.

Collini, S. (2011), From Robbins to McKinsey. *London Review of Books 33*, 16 (August 2011), 9–14.

Crook, D. (1997), Challenge, response and dilution: A revisionist view of the emergency training scheme for teachers, 1945–1951. *Cambridge Journal of Education* 27, 3: 379–389.

Cuban, L. (1999), *How Scholars Trumped Teachers: Constancy and Change in University Curriculum, Teaching, and Research, 1890–1990*. New York, NY: Teachers College Press.

Cuenca, A. (2010), Care, thoughtfulness, and tact: A conceptual framework for university supervisors. *Teaching Education*. 21, 3: 263–278.

Darling-Hammond, L. (2006), *Powerful Teacher Education. Lessons from Exemplary Programs*. San Francisco, CA: Jossey-Bass.

———. (2010), Teacher education and the American future. *Journal of Teacher Education* 61, 1–2: 35–47.

Darling-Hammond, L., Holtzman, D.J., Gatlin, S.J. & Vasquez Heiling, J. (2005), *Does Teacher Preparation Matter? Evidence About Teacher Certification, Teach for America, and Teacher Effectiveness*. Palo Alto, CA: Stanford University.

Davies, A. (1989), *Prin*. London: Samuel French Ltd.

Debord, G. (1977), *Society of the Spectacle*. Detroit, MI: Black and Red.

Dent, H.C. (1977), *The Training of Teachers in England and Wales, 1800–1975*. London: Hodder & Stoughton.

Department for Education (2010), *The Importance of Teaching. The Schools White Paper*. London: DfE.

———. (2011a), *Training Our Next Generation of Outstanding Teachers: A Discussion Paper*. London: DfE.

———. (2011b), *Training Our Next Generation of Outstanding Teachers: Implementation Plan*. London: DfE.

Department of Education and Employment (1997), White Paper: Excellence in Schools, London: Her Majesty's Stationery Office.

———. (1998), Circular 4/98 Teaching: High Status, High Standards: Requirements for Courses of Initial Teacher Training, London: DfEE

Department of Education and Science (DES). (1975), *A Language for Life. [The Bullock Report]. Report of the Committee of Enquiry Appointed by the Secretary of State for Education and Science under the Chairmanship of Sir Alan Bullock FBA*. London: HMSO.

———. (1983), Teaching in Schools: The Content of Initial Training, HMI Discussion paper, London: DES.

———. (1984), *Initial Teacher Training: Approval of Courses (Circular 3/84)*. London: DES.

———. (1992), *Circular No 9/92 Initial Teacher Training (Secondary Phase)*. London: DES.

Dewey, J. (1927), *The Public and Its Problems*. New York, NY: Holt.

Dillabough, J.-A. & Acker, S. (2002), Globalisation, women's work and teacher education: A cross-national analysis. *International Studies in Sociology of Education* 12, 3: 227–260.

Douglas, A. (2009), How Do Secondary School Subject Departments Contribute to the Learning of Student Teachers? PhD thesis submitted to the University of Oxford.

Ducharme, E.R. (1993), *The Lives of Teacher Educators*. New York, NY: Teachers College Press.

Duncan, A. (2011), *Our Future, Our Teachers. The Obama Administration's Plan for Teacher Education Reform and Improvement*. Washington, DC: US Department of Education.

Eagleton, T. (2011), *Why Marx Was Right*. New Haven, CT: Yale University Press.

Earley, P. (1993), Initiation rights? Beginning teachers' professional development and the objectives of induction training, British Journal of In-Service Education, 19, 1, 5–11.

Edwards, A. & Collison, J. (1996), *Mentoring and Developing Practice in Primary Schools*. Buckingham: Oxford University Press.

Edwards, A., Gilroy P. & Hartley D. (2002), *Rethinking Teacher Education. Collaborative Responses to Uncertainty*. London: RoutledgeFalmer.

Elliott, J. (1976–1977), Developing hypotheses about classrooms from teachers' practical constructs: An account of the work of the ford raining project. *Interchange* 7, 2: 2–22.

Ellis, V. (2007), *Subject Knowledge and Teacher Education: The Development of Beginning Teachers' Thinking*. London & New York, NY: Continuum.

———. (2010), Impoverishing experience: The problem of teacher education in England. *Journal of Education for Teaching* 36, 1: 105–120.

———. (2011a), What happened to teachers' knowledge when they played 'the literacy game'?. In Goodwyn, A. & Fuller, C. (Ed.) *The Great Literacy Debate: A Critical Response to the National Literacy Strategy and Framework for English*. London: Routledge.

————. (2011b), Re-energising professional creativity from a CHAT perspective: Seeing knowledge and history in practice. *Mind, Culture and Activity: An International Journal* 18, 2: 181–193.

————. (2012a), Teacher Education in the Public University: The Challenge of Democratising Knowledge Production. Invited presentation to the University of Washington Center for Learning to Teach in Practice, Seattle, 10th April.

————. (2012b), Living with ghosts: 'Disciplines', envy and the future of teacher education. *Changing English: Studies in Culture and Education* 19, 3: 155–166.

————. (2013a), Teacher education in the public university: The challenge of democratising knowledge production. In Wells, G. & Edwards, A. (Eds) *Pedagogy in Higher Education: A Cultural Historical Approach to Learning and Teaching* (pp. 198–214). Cambridge: Cambridge University Press.

————. (2013b), Professional creativity: Towards a collaborative community of teaching. In Sannino, A. & Ellis, V. (Eds) *Learning and Collective Creativity: Activity-Theoretical and Sociocultural Studies*. London & New York, NY: Routledge.

Ellis, V., Blake, A., McNicholl, J. & McNally, J. (2011), The Work of Teacher Education: Final Report. Bristol: ESCalate.

Ellis, V., Edwards, A. & Smagorinsky, P. (Eds) (2010), *Cultural-Historical Perspectives on Teacher Education and Development: Learning Teaching*. London & New York, NY: Routledge.

Ellis, V., McNicholl, J., Blake, A. & McNally, J. (2014), Academic work and proletarianisation: A study of higher education-based teacher educators. *Teaching and Teacher Education* 28, 5: 685–693.

Ellis, V., McNicholl, J. & Pendry, A. (2012), Institutional conceptualisations of teacher education as academic work in England. *Teaching and Teacher Education* 28, 5: 685–693.

Ellis, V. & Orchard, J. (Eds) (2014), *Learning Teaching from Experience: Multiple Perspectives, International Contexts*. London & New York, NY: Bloomsbury.

Elton, L. (2000), The UK research assessment exercise: Unintended consequences. *Higher Education Quarterly* 54, 3: 274–283.

Enders, J. (2000), Academic staff in Europe: Changing employment and working conditions. In Tight, M. (Ed.) *Academic Work and Life: What It Is to Be an Academic, and How This Is Changing* (pp. 7–32). Amsterdam: JAI/Elsevier Science.

Engeström, Y. (1987), *Learning by Expanding: An Activity -Theoretical Approach to Developmental Research*. Helsinki: Orienta-Konsultit.

————. (2007a), Putting activity theory to work: The change laboratory as an application of double stimulation. In Daniels, H., Cole, M. & Wertsch, J.V. (Eds) *The Cambridge Companion to Vygotsky* (pp. 363–382). Cambridge: Cambridge University Press.

————. (2007b), Enriching the theory of expansive learning: lessons from journeys towards coconfiguration. *Mind, Culture and Activity: An International Journal* 41, 1: 23–39.

Engeström, Y., Miettinen, R. & Punamäki, R.L. (Eds) (1999), *Perspectives on Activity Theory*. Cambridge: Cambridge University Press.

Evans, J. Castle, F., Cooper, D., Glatter, R. & Woods, P. (1996), Collaboration: The big new idea for school improbvment. *Journal of Education Policy* 20, 2: 20–38.

Evetts, J. (2009), New professionalism and new public management: Changes, continuities and consequences. *Comparative Sociology* 8: 247–266.

Feiman-Nemser, S., Parker, M. & Zeichner, K. (1993), Are mentor teachers teacher educators? In McIntyre D., Hagger H. & Wilkin M. (Eds) *Mentoring: Perspectives on School-Based Teacher Education*. London: Kogan Page.

Fletcher, S. & Barrett, A. (2004), Developing effective beginning teachers through mentor-based induction. *Mentoring and Tutoring* 51, 1: 17–30.

Flowerdew, L. (2005), An integration of corpus-based and genre-based approaches to text analysis in EAP/ESP: Countering criticisms against corpus-based methodologies. *English for Specific Purposes* 24: 321–332.

Foley, D. (2002), Critical ethnography: The reflexive turn. *Qualitative Studies in Education* 15, 5: 469–490.

Fransson, G. (2010), Mentors assessing mentees? An overview and analyses of the mentorship role concerning newly qualified teachers. *European Journal of Teacher Education* 33, 4: 375–390.

Freebody, P. (2003), *Qualitative Research in Education: Interaction and Practice*. London: Sage.

Furlong, J. (1992), Reconstructing professionalism: Ideological struggle in initial teacher education. In Arnot M. & Barton L. (Eds) *Voicing Concerns: Sociological Perspectives on Contemporary Educational Reforms*. Oxford: Triangle Books.

———. (1996), Re-defining partnership: Revolution or reform in initial teacher education? *Journal of Education for Teaching: International Research and Pedagogy* 22, 1: 39–56.

———. (2009), Partnership, policy and politics: Initial teacher education in England under new labour. In Furlong J., Cochran-Smith M. & Brennan M. (Eds) *Policy and Politics in Teacher Education, International Perspectives*. London and New York, NY: Routledge.

———. (2005), New labour and teacher education: The end of an era? *Oxford Review of Education* 31, 1: 119–134.

———. (2013), *Education – The Anatomy of a Discipline. Rescuing the University Project?* London: Routledge.

———. (2014), The discipline of education: Rescuing the 'university project'. In *Learning to Teach. Part 1: Exploring the History and Role of Higher Education in Teacher Education*. New York, NY: Higher Education Academy.

Furlong, J., Barton, L., Miles, S., Whiting, C. & Whitty, G. (2000), *Teacher Education in Transition: Re-forming Teaching Professionalism*. Buckingham: Open University Press.

Furlong, J. & Lawn, M. (Eds) (2010), *Disciplines of Education: Their Role in the Future of Educational Research*. London: Routledge.

Furlong, J., Cochran-Smith, M. & Brennan, M. (2009a), Introduction. In Furlong, J., Cochran-Smith, M. & Brennan, M. (Eds) *Policy and Politics in Teacher Education, International Perspectives* (pp. 1–7). London: Routledge.

Furlong, J., McNamara, O., Campbell, A., Howson, J. & Lewis, S. (2009b), Partnership, policy and politics: Initial teacher education in England under new labour. In Furlong, J., Cochran-Smith, M. & Brennan, M. (Eds) *Policy and Politics in Teacher Education, International Perspectives* (pp. 45–56). London: Routledge.

Garber, M. (2001), *Academic Instincts*. Princeton, NJ, Princeton University Press.

Gee, J.P. (2003), *What Video Games Have to Teach Us About Learning and Literacy*. London: Palgrave Macmillan.

Gibb, N. (2010), So Who Is Nick Gibb? *Guardian Newspaper*, 17 May 2010, available online: http://www.guardian.co.uk/education/mortarboard/2010/may/17/nick-gibb-upsets-teachers (accessed 24 May 2013).

———. (2014), Teaching unions aren't the problem – Universities are. *The Guardian*. 23 April; available at http://www.theguardian.com/commentisfree/2014/apr/23/teaching-unions-arent-problem-universities-schools-minister (accessed 19 July 2014).

Gibbons, M., Limoges, C., Nowotny, H., Schawrtzman, S., Scott, P. & Trow, M. (1994), *The New Production of Knowledge. The Dynamics of Science and Research in Contemporary Societies*. London: Sage.

Giddens, A. (2000), *The Third Way and Its Critics*. Cambridge: Polity Press.

Givens, N. (2000), Curriculum materials as a vehicle for innovation: A case study of the Nuffield design and technology project. *Research in Science & Technological Education* 18, 1: 71–83.

Goodson, I.F. (2008), *Investigating the Teacher's Life and Work*. Rotterdam: Sense Publishers.

Gosden, P.H.J.H. (1972), *The Evolution of a Profession*. Oxford: Basil Blackwell.

Gove, M. (2012), Raising Standards, Extending Opportunities. Speech to Politeia think-tank. 23 October 2013; available at http://www.politicshome.com/uk/article/64134/raising_standards_extending_opportunities_michael_gove_speech_to_politeia_think_tank_.html (accessed 19 July 2014).

———. (2013), I refuse to surrender to the Marxist teachers hell-bent on destroying our schools. *Daily Mail*. 22nd February; available at http://www.dailymail.co.uk/debate/article-2298146/I-refuse-surrender-Marxist-teachers-hell-bent-destroying-schools-Education-Secretary-berates-new-enemies-promise-opposing-plans.html (accessed 19 July 2014).

Green, J. and Bloome, D. (1997), Ethnography and ethnographers of and in education: A situated perspective'. In Flood, J., Heath, S. & Lapp, D. (Eds) *A Handbook of Research on Teaching Literacy Through the Communicative and Visual Arts* (pp. 181–202). New York, NY: Simon and Shuster Macmillan.

Griffiths, V., Hryniewicz, L. & Thompson, S. (2009), Developing Research Identities: Effective Mentoring for Teacher Educators. Paper presented at the British Educational Research Association annual conference, Manchester; available at http://www.leeds.ac.uk/educol/documents/189278.pdf (accessed 2 February 2013).

Grossman, P., Hammerness, K. & McDonald, M. (2009), Redefining teaching, re-imagining teacher education. *Teachers and Teaching* 15, 2: 273–290.

Guillory, J. (1994), Literary critics as intellectuals: Class analysis and the crisis of the humanities. In Dimock, W.-C. & Gilmore, M.T. (Eds) *Rethinking Class: Literary Studies and Social Formations* (pp. 107–149). New York, NY: Columbia University Press.

Gutiérrez, K. & Penuel, W. (2014), Relevance to practice as a criterion for rigor. *Educational Researcher* (Jan/Feb) 43: 19–23.

Gutmann, A. (1999), *Democratic Education*. Princeton, NJ: Princeton University Press.

Guyton, E. & McIntyre, D.J. (1990), Student teaching and school experiences. In Houston W.R. (Ed.) *Handbook of Research on Teacher Education.* New York, NY: Macmillan, 514–534.

Halliday, M.A.K. (1975), *Learning How to Mean.* London: Edward Arnold.

Harvey, D. (2005), *A Brief History of Neoliberalism.* Oxford: Oxford University Press.

———. (2010), *A Companion to Marx's Capital.* London & New York, NY: Verso.

Hazlehurst, S., Morris, B. & Wiliam, D. (2010), National Financial Implications of RAE 2008 Outcomes. Supplementary Report. London/Macclesfield: UCET/BERA; available at http://www.bera.ac.uk/files/2010/07/BERA-UCET-RAE-Report-June-2010.pdf (accessed 30 July 2010).

Heath, S.B. (1983), *Ways with Words: Language and Life in Communities and Classrooms.* Cambridge: Cambridge University Press.

Heath, S.B. & Street, B. (2007), *On Ethnography: Approaches to Language and Literacy Research. National Conference on Research in Language and Literacy.* New York, NY: Teachers College, Columbia University.

Hester, S. & Eglin, P. (1997), *Culture in Action: Studies in Membership Categorization Analysis.* Washington, DC: University of America Press.

Higher Education Funding Council for England (HEFCE) (2009a), *Research Assessment Exercise 2008: Summary Statistics Panel K*; available at http://www.rae.ac.uk/pubs/2009/ov/ (accessed 2 February 2013).

———. (2009b), *Research Assessment Exercise 2008: Sub-panel 45 Education. Subject Overview Report*; available at http://www.rae.ac.uk/pubs/2009/ov/ (accessed 2 February 2013).

Higher Education Statistics Agency (HESA) (2009), *Resources of Higher Education Institutions.* Cheltenham: Author.

Hirsch, E.D. (2013), A wealth of words. The key to increasing upward mobility is expanding vocabulary. *City Journal* 23, 1 (Winter 2013); available at http://www.city-journal.org/2013/23_1_vocabulary.html (accessed 19 July 2014).

Hobson, A.J. (2002), Student teachers' perceptions of school-based mentoring in initial teacher training. *Mentoring and Tutoring: Partnership in Learning* 10, 1: 5–10.

Holmwood, J. (Ed.) (2011), *A Manifesto for the Public University.* London: Bloomsbury Academic.

Hopper, B. (2001), The role of the HEI tutor in initial teacher education school-based placements. *Mentoring and Tutoring: Partnership in Learning.* 9, 3: 211–222.

Horner, B. (2000), *Terms of Work for Composition: A Materialist Critique.* Albany, NY: State University of New York Press.

Hutchinson, S. (2008), Boundaries, Bricolage and Student-Teacher Learning, PhD thesis submitted to then Open University.

Hymes, D. (1973), On communicative competence. In Pride, J.B. & Homes, J. (Eds) *Sociolinguistics.* Harmondsworth: Penguin.

Ingleby, E. & Tummons, J. (2012), Repositioning professionalism: Teachers, mentors, policy and praxis. *Research in Post-Compulsory Education* 17, 2: 1673–178.

International Alliance of Leading Education Institutes (IALEI) (2008), *Transforming Teacher Education: Redefined Professionals for 21st Century Schools.* Singapore: National Institute of Education.

Iven, H. (1994), Teachers should be trained in partnership. *Teaching Today* Spring: 24–25.

Jonçich Clifford, G. & Guthrie, J. W. (1988), Ed School. A Brief for Professional Education. Geraldine. University of Chicago Press, Chicago.

Jones, M. (2001), Mentors' perceptions of their roles in school-based teacher training in England and Germany. *Journal of Education for Teaching: International research and pedagogy* 27, 1: 75–94.

Kirk, G. (1999), The passing of monotechnic teacher education in Scotland. *Scottish Educational Review* 31, 2: 100–111.

Kosnik, C. & Beck, C. (2008), In the shadows: Non-tenure-line instructors in pre-service teacher education. *European Journal of Teacher Education* 31, 2: 185–202.

Koerner, M., Rust, F. & Baumgartner, F. (2002), Exploring roles in student teaching placements. *Teacher Education Quarterly* 29, 2: 35–58.

Labaree, D. (2004), *The Trouble with Ed Schools.* New Haven, CT: Yale University Press.

Lakoff, G. (2004), *Don't Think of An Elephant! Know Your Values and Frame the Debate – The Essential Guide for Progressives.* New York, NY: Chelsea Green Publishing.

Lampert, M. (2009), Learning teaching in, from and for practice: What do we mean? *Journal of Teacher Education* 61, 1–2: 21–34.

Lave, J. (1988), Cognition in practice: Mind, mathematics, and culture in everyday life. Cambridge University Press, Cambridge

Lave, J. & Wenger, E. (1991), *Situated Learning: Legitimate Peripheral Participation.* Cambridge: Cambridge University Press.

Lawn, M. & Ozga, J. (1988), The educational worker: A reassessment of teachers. In Ozga J. (Ed.) *School Work.* Milton Keynes: Open University Press.

Lemov, D. (2010), Reflection and Practice. In Teach Like a Champion (pp257–259). Hoboken, NJ: Jossey-Bass.

Leont'ev, A.N. (1978), *Activity, Consciousness and Personality.* Englewood Cliffs, NJ: Prentice Hall.

Lipman, P. (2011), *The New Political Economy of Urban Education: Neoliberalism, Race and the Right to the City.* New York, NY: Routledge.

Liston, D. P. (1995), Work in teacher education: A current assessment of U.S. teacher education. In Shimahara N. & Holowinsky I. (Eds) *Teacher Education in Industrialised Nations* (pp. 87–124). New York, NY: Garland Publishing.

Lye, C. & Vernon, J. (2011), The Humanities and the Crisis of the Public University. In The Newsletter of the Townsend Center for the Humanities at the University of California Berkeley (February/March 2011). Retrieved from http://townsendcenter.berkeley.edu/pubs/TC_Newsletter_FebMarch_2011.pdf

MacDougall, L., Mtika, P., Reid, I. & Weir, D. (2013), Enhancing feedback in student-teacher field experiences in Scotland: The role of school-university partnership. *Professional Development in Education* 39, 3: 420–437.

Maguire, M. (1993), *The Job of Educating Teachers.* Unpublished PhD thesis. Centre for Educational Studies, King's College, London.

———. (2000), Inside/outside the ivory tower: Teacher education in the English academy. *Teaching in Higher Education* 5, 149–166.

Maguire, M. & Weiner, G. (1994), The place of women in teacher education: Discourses of power. *Educational Review* 46, 2: 121–139.

Mahony, P., & I. Hextall. (2000). Reconstructing teaching: Standards, performance and accountability. London: Routledge Falmer.

Mäkitalo, Å. & Saljo, R. (2003), Talk in context and context in talk. The use and meaning of members' categories in institutional discourse. *Text* 22, 1: 57–82.

Mandlebaum, D.G. (1973), The study of life history: Gandhi. *Current Anthropology* 14, 3: 177–206.

Marginson, S. & Considine, M. (2000), Markets in education, Cambridge University Press.

Marginson, S. (2010), Rethinking academic work in the global era. *Journal of Higher Education Policy and Management* 22, 1: 23–35.

Martin, R. (1997), Academic labor: An introduction. *Social Text* 51 (Summer), 1–8.

Martin D.M. & Peim, N.A. (2009), Critical perspectives on activity theory. *Educational Review* 61, 2: 131–138.

Martin, S.D., Snow, J.L. & Franklin Torrez, C.A. (2011), Navigating the terrain of third space: Tensions with/in relationships in school-university partnerships. *Journal of Teacher Education* 62: 299–311.

Marx, K. (1887/1992), *Capital: A Critique of Political Economy*. Volume 1. (B. Fowkes, Trans). London: Penguin Classics.

Marx, K. & Engels, F. (1845–1846/1964), *The German Ideology in Collected Works Volume 5: Marx and Engels: 1845–1847*. (S. Ryazanskaya, Trans.). Moscow: Progress Publishers.

———. (1888/2008), *The Communist Manifesto*. Ware: Wordsworth Editions.

Maynard, P. (1996), The limits of mentoring: The contribution of the higher education tutor to primary student teachers' school-based learning. In Furlong J. & Smith R. (Eds) *The Role of Higher Education in Initial Teacher Training*. London: Kogan Page.

Maynard, T. (2000), Learning to teach or learning to manage mentors? Experiences of school-based teacher training. *Mentoring and Tutoring: Partnership in Learning* 8, 1: 17–30.

Maynard, T. & Furlong, J. (1993), Learning to teach and models of mentoring. In Kerry T. & Shelton Mayes A. (Eds) *Issues in Mentoring*. Milton Keynes: Open University.

McEnery, T. & Wilson, A. (2001), *Corpus Linguistics: An Introduction*. Second edition. Edinburgh: Edinburgh University Press.

McLaughlin, K., Osborne, S.P. & Ferlie, W. (2002), *New Public Management: Current Trends and Future Prospects*. London & New York, NY: Routledge.

McNicholl, J. & Blake, A. (2013), Transforming teacher education: an activity theory analysis, *Journal of Education for Teaching: International Research and Pedagogy* 39, 3: 281–300.

McNicholl, J., Ellis, V. & Blake, A. (2013), Introduction to the special issue on the work of teacher education: Policy, practice and institutional conditions. *Journal of Education for Teaching: International Research and Pedagogy* 39, 3: 260–265.

Menter, I., Brisard E. & Smith, I. (2006), *Covergence or Divergence? Initial Teacher Education in Scotland and England*. Edinburgh: Dunedin Academic Press.

Menter, I. (2011), Four 'academic sub-tribes'; but one territory? Teacher educators and teacher education in Scotland. *Journal of Education for Teaching: International Research and Pedagogy* 37, 3: 293–308.

Mercer, N. (2000), *Words and Minds: How We Use Language to Think Together*. London: Routledge.

Miettinen, R. (2013), *Innovation, Human Capabilities and Democracy: Towards an Enabling Welfare State*. Oxford: Oxford University Press.

Mills, D., Jepson, A., Coxon, T., Easterby-Smith, M., Hawkins, P. & Spencer, J. (2006), *Demographic Review of the UK Social Sciences*. Swindon: Economic and Social Research Council.

Moffett, J. (1968), *Teaching the Universe of Discourse*. Boston, MA: Houghton Mifflin.

Montague, W. (1987), Administrators Rebut Bennett's Critique of Burgeoning Bureaucratic 'Blob'. *Education Week*. 9th September; available at http://www.edweek.org/ew/articles/1987/09/09/07200023.h07.html (accessed 19 July, 2014).

Moran, A.J., Dallat, J. & Abbott, J. (1999), Newly qualified teachers in post-primary schools in Northern Ireland: The support provided for their needs and their own vision for induction. *European Journal of Teacher Education* 22, 2/3: 173–189.

Moyles, J. & Stuart, D. (2003), Which school-based elements of partnership in initial teacher training in the UK support trainee teachers' professional development? In *Research Evidence in Education Library*. London: EPPI-Centre, Social Science Research Unit, Institute of Education.

Murray, J. (2005), Addressing the priorities: New teacher educators and induction into higher education. *Journal of Teacher Education* 28, 1: 67–85.

———. (2007), Countering insularity in teacher education: Academic work on pre-service courses in nursing, social work and teacher education. *Journal of Education for Teaching: International Research and Pedagogy* 33, 3: 261–291.

Murray, J., Campbell, A., Hextall, I, Hulme, M., Jones, M., Menter, I., Procter, R. & Wall, K. (2009), Research and teacher education in the UK: Building capacity. *Teaching and Teacher Education* 25, 7: 944–950.

Murray, J. & Kosnik, C. (2011), Academic work and identities in teacher education. *Journal of Education for Teaching: International Research and Pedagogy* 37, 3: 243–246.

Murray, J. & Male, T. (2005), Becoming a teacher educator: Evidence from the field. *Teaching and Teacher Education* 21, 2: 125–142.

Musset, P. (2010), Initial Teacher Education and Continuing Training Policies in Comparative Perspective: Current Practices in OECD Countries and a Literature Review on Potential Effects. OECD Working Paper No. 48. Paris: OECD Publishing.

Nelson, S.R., Leffler, J.C. & Hansen, B.A. (2009), *Toward a Research Agenda for Understanding and Improving the Use of Research Evidence*. Portland, OR: Northwest Regional Educational Laboratory. Retrieved from http://educationnorthwest.org/resource/694

Nguyen, H.T. (2009), An inquiry-based practicum model: What knowledge, practices, and relationships typify empowering teaching and learning experiences for student teachers, cooperating teachers and college supervisors? *Teaching and Teacher Education* 25: 655–662.

Nowotny, H., Scott, P. & Gibbons, M. (2003), 'Mode 2' revisited: The new production of knowledge. *Minerva* 41; 179–194.

Nuttall, J., Brennan, M., Zipin, L., Tuinamuana, K. & Cameron, L. (2013), Teacher education as academic work: Insights from Australian universities. *JET: Journal of Education for Teaching* 39, 3: 329–343.

OECD (2005), *Teachers Matter: Attracting, Developing and Retaining Effective Teachers*. Paris: OECD.

———. (2011a), *Building a High Quality Teaching Profession: Lessons from Round the World*. Paris: OECD Publishing.

———. (2011b), *Lessons from PISA for the United States, Strong Performers and Successful Reformers in Education*. Paris: OECD Publishing.

Office for Standards in Education (Ofsted) (2007), *Narrowing the Gap. The Inspection of Children's Services*. London: Ofsted.

Ogborn, J. & Whitehouse, M. (Ed.) (2000), *Advancing Physics AS*. Bristol: Institute of Physics Publishing.

———. (Ed.) (2001), *Advancing Physics A2*. Bristol: Institute of Physics Publishing.

Ogborn, J. (2002), Ownership and transformation: Teachers using curriculum innovations. *Physics Education* 37, 2: 142–146.

Olsen, B. (2008), *Teaching What They Learn, Learning What They Live: How Teachers' Personal Histories Shape Their Professional Development*. Boulder, CO: Paradigm Publishers.

Pickard, S. (2014), Higher Education in the UK and the US.

Popkewitz, T. (1998), *Struggling for the Soul: The Politics of Schooling and the Construction of the Teacher*. New York, NY: Teachers College Press.

Popper, K. (1945), *The Open Society and Its Enemies*. Vol. 1. London: Routledge.

Protherough, R. & Pick, J. (2002), *Managing Britannia. Culture and Management in Modern Britain*. Exeter: The Brynmill Press.

Reeves, J. & Boreham, N. (2006), What's in a vision? Introducing an organisational learning strategy in a local education authority's service. *Oxford Review of Education* 32, 4: 467–486.

Research Excellence Framework (REF) (2011), *Decisions on Assessing Research Impact*. Bristol: REF.

Rhoades, G. & Slaughter, S. (1997), Academic capitalism, managed professionals and supply-side higher education. *Social Text* 51 (Summer 1997), 9–38.

Rich, H. & Hannafin, B. (2008), Capturing and assessing evidence of student teacher inquiry: A case study. *Teaching and Teacher Education* 24, 6: 1426–1440.

Rippon, J.H. & Martin, M. (2006), *Teaching and Teacher Education* 22: 84–99.

Ryder, J. & Banner, I. (2011), Multiple aim in the development of a major reform of the national curriculum for science in England. *International Journal of Science Education* 33, 5: 709–725.

Sahlberg, P. (2011), *Finnish Lessons: What Can the World Learn from Educational Change in Finland?*. New York, NY: Teachers College Press.

Saltman, K. (2010), *The Gift of Education: Public Education and Venture Philanthropy*. New York, NY: Palgrave Macmillan.

Schuster, J.H. & Finkelstein, M.J. (2008), *The American Faculty: The Restructuring of Academic Work and Careers*. Baltimore, MD: The Johns Hopkins University Press.

Seddon, T., Ozga, J. & Levin, J.S. (2013), Global transitions and teacher professionalism. In Seddon, T. & Levin, J.S. (Eds) *World Yearbook of Education 2013. Educators, Professionalism and Politics: Global Transitions, National Spaces and Professional Projects.* London: Routledge.

Skilbeck, M. (1990), *Curriculum Reform: An Overview of Trends.* Paris: OECD.

Slaughter, S. & Leslie, L.L. (1997), *Academic Capitalism: Politics, Policies, and the Entrepreneurial University.* Baltimore, MD: The Johns Hopkins University Press.

Slaughter, S. & Rhoades, G. (2004), *Academic Capitalism and the New Economy: Markets, State and Higher Education.* Baltimore, MD: The Johns Hopkins University Press.

Sleeter, C. (2014), Toward teacher education research that informs policy. *Educational Researcher* (April) 43: 46–153

Slick, S.K. (1997), Assessing versus assisting: The supervisor's role in the complex dynamics of the student teaching triad. *Teaching and Teacher Education*, 13: 713–726.

Smagorinsky, P., Cook, L.S. & Johnson, T.S. (2003), The twisting path of concept development in learning to teach. *Teachers College Record* 105: 1399–1436

Smith, M.E. (2000), The role of the tutor in initial teacher education. *Mentoring and Tutoring: Partnership in Learning* 8, 2: 137–144.

Stenhouse, L. (1968), The humanities curriculum project. *Journal of Curriculum Studies* 1, 1: 26–33.

Street, B.V. (1984), *Literacy in Theory and Practice.* Cambridge: Cambridge University Press.

Swennen, A. & van der Klink, K. (2009), *Becoming a Teacher Educator: Theory and Practice for Teacher Educators.* Dordrecht: Springer.

Taylor, W. (1969), *Society and the Education of Teachers.* London: Faber and Faber.

The University of Newcastle (2008), *Celebrating 60 Years of Teacher Education: School of Education, The University of Newcastle.* Callaghan: The University of Newcastle.

Tierney, W.G. (2001), Faculty of education in a period of systemic reform. In Tierney, W.G. (Ed.) *Faculty Work in Schools of Education: Rethinking Roles and Rewards for the Twenty-first Century* (pp. 79–102). Albany, NY: State University of New York Press.

Tight, M. (2004), Introduction: Higher education as a field of research. In Tight, M. (Ed.) *The RoutledgeFalmer Reader in Higher Education.* London: RoutledgeFalmer.

Tillema, H.H. (2009), Assessment of learning to teach: Appraisal of practice teaching lessons by mentors, supervisors, and student teachers. *Journal of Teacher Education*, 60: 155–167.

Timperley, H., Wilson, A, Barrar, H. & Fung, L. (2007), Teacher Professional Learning and Development: Best Evidence Synthesis Iteration [BES]. Wellington, New Zealand: Ministry of Education.

Tocqueville, A.de. (1969/1848), *Democracy in America.* Trans. G. Lawrence. Cambridge, MA: Doubleday and Co.

Tomlinson, P.D. (1998), Teacher education and psychologies of skills. In Shorrocks-Taylor, D. (Ed.) *Directions in Educational Psychology.* London: Whurr Publishers.

Toom, A., Kynäslathi, H., Krokford, L., Jyrhämä, R., Stenberg, K., Maaranen, K. & Kansanen, P. (2010), Experiences of a research-based approach to teacher education: Suggestions for future policies. *European Journal of Education* 45, 2 (II): 331–344.

Training and Development Agency for Training and Schools, TDA (2009), ITT place allocations 2008/09-2010/11, available at http://www.tda.gov.uk/partners/funding/allocations/allocations0809.aspx (accessed 21 January 2010).

Tuchman, G. (2009), *Wannabe U: Inside the Corporate University*. Chicago, IL: University of Chicago Press.

Turner, S.E. (2001), The evolving production functions of schools of education. In Tierney W.G. (Ed.) *Faculty Work in Schools of Education: Rethinking Roles and Rewards for the Twenty-First Century*. Albany, NY: State University of New York Press.

Twombly, S. B., Wolf-Wendel, L., Williams, J. & Green, P. (2006), Searching for the next generation of teacher educators: Assessing the success of academic searches. *Journal of Teacher Education* 57, 5: 498–511.

Universities UK (2013), *Parliamentary Briefing. Initial Teacher Training*. 7 November. London: Universities UK.

Valencia, S. W., Martin, S.D., Place, N.A. & Grossman, P. (2009), Complex interactions in student teaching: Lost opportunities for learning. *Journal of Teacher Education* 60, 3: 304–322.

Valsiner, J. & van der Veer, R. (2000), *The Social Mind: Construction of the Idea*. Cambridge: Cambridge University Press.

Vygotsky, L.S., Cole, M., John-Steiner, V., Scribner, S. & Souberman, E. (Eds) (1978), *Mind in Society* Cambridge, MA: Harvard University Press.

———. (1986), *Thought and Language*. (A. Kozulin, Ed. & Trans.). Cambridge, MA: MIT Press.

Walkerdine, V. (1988), *The Mastery of Reason: Cognitive Development and the Production of Rationality*. London & New York, NY: Routledge.

Walzer, M. (1981), Philosophy and democracy. *Political Theory* 9, 3: 379–399.

White, E. (2014), Being a teacher and a teacher educator – Developing a new identity? *Professional Development in Education* 40, 3: 436–449.

Whitty, G., Furlong, J., Barton, L, Miles, S. & Whiting, C. (2007), Training in turmoil: Researching initial teacher education in England in the 1990s. In Freeman-Moir J. & Scott A. (Eds) *Shaping the Future: Critical Essays on Teacher Education*. Rotterdam: Sense.

Williams, A. & Soares, A. (2000), The roles of higher education in the initial training of secondary school teachers: The views of the key participants. *Journal of Education for Teaching: International Research and Pedagogy* 26, 3: 225–244.

Willis, P. (2000), *The Ethnographic Imagination*. Oxford: Blackwell Publishers Ltd.

Yusko, B. & Feiman-Nemser, S. (2008), Embracing contraries: Combining assistance and assessment in new teacher induction. *Tecaher College Record* 110, 5: 923–953.

Zeichner, K. & Liston, D. (1990), Traditions of reform in US teacher education. *Journal of Teacher Education* 41, 2: 3–20.

Zeichner, K. (2009), Teacher Education and the Struggle for Social Justice. New York: Routledge.

Zeichner, K. (2010), Rethinking the connections between campus courses and field experiences in college- and university-based teacher education. *Journal of Teacher Education* 61: 89–99.

Zeichner, K., Payne, K. & Brayko, K. (2012), *Democratising Knowledge in University Teacher Education Through Practice-Based Methods Teaching and Mediated Field Experiences in Schools and Communities. Issue Paper 12-1.* Seattle: University of Washington Center for the Study of Learning to Teach in Practice.

Zeichner, K. & Sandoval, C.P. (2013), Venture Philanthropy and Teacher Education Policy in the US: The Role of the New Schools Venture Fund. Paper presented at the annual meeting of the American Educational Research Association, San Francisco, April 2013.

Index